C000180259

SPIRIT INSPIRATIONS

BY

DENISE PILGRIM

CON-PSY PUBLICATIONS MIDDLESEX

First Edition

© Denise Pilgrim
2006

This book is copyrighted under the Berne Convention. All rights reserved.
No part of this book may be reproduced or utilised in any form or by any
means, electronic or mechanical, including photocopying, recording,
or by any information storage and retrieval system, without permission in
writing from the publisher. Except for the purpose of reviewing or criticism,
as permitted under the Copyright Act of 1956.

Published by

CON-PSY PUBLICATIONS

P.O. BOX 14, GREENFORD, MIDDLESEX, UB6 0UF.

ISBN 978 1 898680 43 7

INDEX

FOREWORD

This book has been written for use in churches and for the comfort of individuals, who are seeking spiritual comfort and knowledge. When a short reading is required in church services, this book is ideal. When the problems of life become overwhelming and threaten to overpower your self worth, just pick up this book and turn to the appropriate page. Each reading can be a tool to help you to get through those difficult times, the words can help you to rise above your troubles giving you that extra strength of endurance and strength and proving that the power of spirit is at work in your life.

All these readings were spirit inspired and I give thanks to all those in spirit that used me as a voice. My search for truth and knowledge of spirit continues and with their love and continued help, I trust that these words will reach and inspire those in need of healing and upliftment.

Denise Pilgrim

SPIRITUAL ENLIGHTENMENT

There is in this world today, a hope and a longing for things to improve. There is hope that one day mankind will understand, that we are all brothers and sisters in spirit, that we all come from the same source, and are spirit inhabiting physical bodies for a short time, until we discard this physical overcoat and return to that land of light and love.

We who have experienced spirit communication, know that this is a truth and a fact, but there are those who have not yet come upon this knowledge, either because their religion forbids it's investigation, or because their lifestyle has not given them time for thought, either way, this knowledge has yet to be acquired.

What will be their experience at the end of their earthly sojourn? What a surprise they will have when they make that transition. In absolute wonder, they will open their eyes in a new world, the adjustment taking a longer or shorter time, according to their ability to understand the change. Will they say "if only I had known, I'd have lived my life differently", or will they say, "why didn't somebody tell me, I'd have been much kinder"

There is great responsibility that comes with the knowledge of survival of physical death, for those of us who do know, cannot say I didn't know. With this knowledge and responsibility also comes a greater penalty, for when you act in ignorance, you may be looked upon with sympathy, but when you act with knowledge of the spiritual wrongs that you do, you cause yourself much pain and your knowledge and understanding of your actions will judge you, no one else.

Our hope is that the knowledge of survival of the spirit, will be made known to every man, so that there will be no surprises at the end, but fulfilled expectations, without the fear of the age old ideas to hold us back from our spiritual progress.

We all at one time or another pray that spiritual enlightenment will come upon those in most need, our friends in spirit indeed have their work cut out in their endeavours to achieve this, but they cannot do it alone, they need willing and able workers here on the earth plane in order to do this, in the simplest ways that you can imagine, your knowledge and understanding of spirit, immediately qualifies you as a channel and a worker for spirit, the more knowledge you have, the closer spirit will come and use your knowledge for the sake of mankind. Learn as much as you can about the truths of spirit, and with the joint effort of this world and the next, love and understanding of each other and nations, can become more than a dream.

HARMONY

Let everything you do and say, have meaning. If everything you do and say comes from the goodness of your heart, then you will know that you are living your life in the best way that you can.

This life, is not judged by any outside personality other than yourself, but self. Judgment is brought into play, as is the inner knowing of right and wrong at any given time. There are times, when you just know that something said or done is right, for you feel it, and there are times when you just know something is wrong, for you feel it, your judgment is there all the time.

In life there always seems to be two sides of the coin, heads or tales, but sometimes there seems to be a grey area of which there is no certain answer to a question. It seems to be right there around the edge of that coin. When this uncertainty arises, you need to use your intuition, this sense, the sixth sense, has been given to you for good reason and should be used more often. It exists in order that you can save yourself from making grave errors in your life, and has saved many people from making decisions that can be harmful to others as well as to the self.

In order to live as the divine spirit intended us to live, there must be harmony in our lives, and this comes from right thinking and consequently right doing. None of us live totally alone, we live in a world full of people, and harmony is the only way that life can progress into a fullness of happiness as an experience.

In our working life we get paid money as thanks for doing our daily jobs, in our lives we should expect happiness as a result of the working of harmony in our daily lives, that is the result and proper payment that is due to each and every one of us as payment in full for our services, that is what a life of right living should pay out as dividends. Ah! but, you say, I am not always happy, and I live and think aright every day of my life, so this law of spirit must somehow have a flaw in it, it does not work, for my actions should always benefit myself first and then others, I should be able to save myself from pain.

The law of harmony encompasses all, in order to have harmony, you need another to harmonise with in joining together, self must always come last for harmony to work, it embraces all who seek it and stays away from those who reject it. It's partner is peace, and hand in hand mankind too must walk together, then harmony, peace, love and contentment will become the only coin and treasure that you need and will receive.

I AM NOT GONE

I am not in the graveyard,
Ashes or dust,
Nor laid in a coffin
'Til the trumpet sounds must
Call me forth on judgment day
To account for my life in such a way
That to heaven or hell I must go,
For if I've been bad, He will know.

But by your side is where I stand,
Often, so often I touch your hand,
I feel your tears when you cry,
And wonder "how now will I get by?"

You ache to talk to me again,
To hear my voice, just once again,
Just one more hug, one last embrace,
To say "I love you" to my face.

Your pain and sorrow draws me closer,
My love for you now ten times stronger,
Be still and calm and mind at rest,
For it is in that silence that I speak best.

Then you will know that I am not gone,
That life never ends and love goes on,
To become much stronger and greater in force,
Than it ever could be while I was on earth.

The veil that separates us is oh so thin,
If you realised this then you would begin,
To smile at life instead of frowning,
And live for today instead of yearning,
For opportunities past and doors that never opened,
Reflection is good but letting go gives you freedom,
To open other doors behind which you will find,
A whole new life waiting to be lived and enjoyed.

BECOME A POSITIVE FORCE

Each and every one of you is a child of God, created by the Divine Spirit in love and wisdom, not by any kind of mistake or accident, but with purpose, reason and meaning.

Each of you have a spirit and a soul, with a destiny that lies before you, seemingly unknown, but there nevertheless. With each thought, deed and action, you develop your soul, and your destiny can be altered in a positive or negative way, according to the way you think, for what you view as negative usually has a positive outcome in the long run.

The power that created you knows your strengths and your weaknesses, and smiles upon you when both are demonstrated, for a parent always watches his children, with pride and knowledge, knowing that they grow through experience and sometimes frustration. We are children of many colours, but connected by the same spirit. It saddens us all when we cannot live side by side in peace, but we continue to have hope, in the knowledge that we can turn to our creator without fear, and be loved unconditionally, for the love of a parent for his child is the strongest of all loves.

You cannot ever be alone, for that would mean that you have been forgotten, and the wisdom and love of which I speak, cannot make a mistake, you are in the hands and charge of those unseen but real, who have a duty to watch and care and guide you throughout your earthly life, and let us not forget those who, when they were here in the physical body, had a blood bond with you also, and still continue that bond of love whilst in the world of spirit, there is no disconnection because of physical death.

No, you cannot be alone, for love is all embracing, and reaches even those who wish to hide themselves away, in time, even they will see that their loneliness was a misguided thought. So keep your thoughts positive as often as you can, when those negative thoughts threaten to fill your mind, actively push them away, you are strong enough to achieve this, and anything that you wish to achieve in your life.

Your thoughts and ideas of a positive future for yourself will fan out and touch and affect others, in this way you become a teacher for others, and as you teach, those listening and watching will follow in your positive footsteps, and the chain reaction will continue.

We who were all created in love as children of the Divine Spirit, let us join together and become a positive force in the lives of others and the world.

CHANGE......AT THE RIGHT TIME

Let your mind open up to the truths of spirit that exist and abound about your daily lives. Let the love of spirit enter your life and remain, ever creating the harmony that is so needed and wanting in your lives.

There are a million different examples of spirit working for harmony in your life, but you close your eyes to them and do not see their precious working or values. It is we know, very hard for you to enjoy and appreciate something that is not always physical, but is sometimes surreal and as gentle as a feather, but always there is an essence left behind, that is tangible enough for you to sense in some way.

Spirit have been at work when the new life of spring begins to show forth it's beauty in the way you experience it every year at this time, but it has also been at work in your life, when a new journey for you begins, or a new pathway in your life suddenly appears. A new idea suddenly emerges in your mind and you wonder that you never thought of this before. Spirit are working in your life. Every change that happens to you and your nearest and dearest, has occurred with the help of your loved ones in spirit.

You cannot ask spirit for a car, and have it drop out of the sky at your feet, for this is not how they work, but in time, the right connections will be made and all will fall into place to bring about this event, at the right time, and the right time will be the time in your life, when you can safely manage this vehicle, because of your own spiritual and mental being. There are many faculties that have to be taken into consideration before an event can take place at the right time. As there is a time for all seasons, know that there is a time for all events in your life, and if you are waiting for something that you may have prayed for or asked spirit to help you with, understand that the time may not be right for this prayer to be answered, for when you are asking for something to happen, another may be asking for it not to happen, and spirit best work when there is harmony.

Take that walk in the park or the country that you keep promising yourself, and clear the cobwebs from your mind, then the situation which you wish to change, will become much clearer to you, and you may see that it was not the situation that needed to change, but clarity of mind to handle it, and to be able to see it clearly from all angles.

God does work in mysterious ways, and through His divine angels performs many wonders, in the universe and in personal lives. The pathway you presently walk, is right for you now on many levels, change will come when you are ready and the many facets of life's diamond are in harmony.

EACH MOMENT IS A PRECIOUS GIFT

There is a need for each and every one of us to realise that this life that we live, is only temporary. We wake up each day, and our lives are full of different events, things that we have done, said and thought, but whilst living each moment of our day, we tend to forget that each moment, though real to us, is only a moment in eternity, that may never again be repeated or experienced again in that way.

It is time to live as though each moment, hour or day, is the most precious gift that can be received, for life in this world is only temporary. None of us know how long we have to spend on this earth plane, but we know that even 80 years is not a long time, when you think of the long years you have ahead of you living in the world of spirit. You need to try and make your life now as colourful and meaningful as you can, so that your future life may become more so. This life as a spirit being, will one day become a distant and past memory. It will become a once upon a time story that you may or may not want to recall and tell to others, and maybe even use as an example or for teaching, but in every way, it will be your experience and your personal truth, that you will carry with you always.

Let your life lived become a shining example to others. There will be times and events in your life that you will not want to share as an example with others, but even those times that did not make you proud, can be used by others as examples of milestones to avoid or to show the workings of cause and effect. Life in the physical body, and on the physical earth plane is not an easy one to live, we all know that, but looked at in its entirety, you will see that there has been a balance struck, and that you did the best you could with what you had, and that the good you did, far outweighed the bad. In this light, you will also realise that the struggles which seemed to be many, led you quite nicely into avenues of work or styles of living, that you would never consciously have thought of doing, for every struggle and heartache that you experience, is a road to something bigger and better for you.

Your worst experiences are your graduation times to the higher classes of learning. If you look at the most beautiful and most scented rose, you will pick that beautiful flower and find that on its stem are sharp thorns, you cannot have a lifetime of bliss without the occasional thunderstorm, for of what benefit would that be to you. The strength and worthiness of the iron, depends very much on the hardening and preparation in the furnace, then all can see your strength and worth.

This life is only temporary, but how you live can and will be your eternal medal of victory and achievement.

YOUR FUTURE IS BRIGHT

It is now generally known that this earthly life is but a preparation for a future life, in a world where it is known that love reigns supreme and that even there, lessons are still to be learnt.

In that world of light, there is still plenty of knowledge left to be acquired, and this knowledge is made available to those whose minds are ready to receive. There will never be a time when there is nothing left to learn. It is much the same here, we learn daily, whether we are aware of this or not, yet, we tell ourselves that our minds cannot learn anything new when we feel we have reached a certain age, or that what we learn is of little significance. We forget that our subconscious minds miss nothing.

Your friends in spirit had the same problems that you now endure, and they are always willing to help when asked, it is their joy when they see us endure and conquer our problems, they help to smooth the path for us, but the hard work and sometimes heartache comes from us, resulting most of the time in a strengthening of the spirit within, for once deep sadness and heartache has touched us, we are never quite the same as we were prior to that occasion, and we go from strength to strength, fighting our earthly battles, winning some and seemingly to lose others, but you see, you never lose, you can only gain from experiences, hard as some of those experiences may have been to cope with, during your sadness the veil between this world and the spirit world became much thinner, they drew closer to you, soothing you, healing you and giving you strength.

Whatever you endure in this physical life, know that the Divine Spirit never allows any of us to go through our difficult experiences alone, for love reigns supreme, it is the one key that can open every box, it is the one thing that can soothe every pain and dry every tear, this applies in both worlds, in fact the two worlds are one, if we only but realise it, help is never far away.

Use the strength given to you to rise above every situation that threatens to drag you down, after all you are spirit first and physical body second, you are light, you can never die, eternity stretches before you, with many adventures to come.

Steel yourself and put a smile on your face, for the future is brighter than you can know, and it eagerly awaits your coming with a welcoming anticipation.

The end of physical life here on earth, brings about the beginning of eternal life in the world of spirit. This is a knowledge and a fact that most of you now understand, it is a fact that you can use to uplift and comfort those that are in need, and are in mourning for their loved ones who have passed out of this life into the next. This knowledge can ease the pain of physical bereavement, for to know that your loved one is no longer in the pain that you witnessed before their eyes close on this physical life, and to know that their new life now begins, helps you greatly in your hour of need.

For that person now in spirit there is ahead of them, spiritual progression, if they desire it, for free will does not end at death's door, free will is continuous and nobody is compelled to learn or improve their spiritual nature if they have no desire to do so.

As is here on earth, if you have no wish to learn of spiritual truths and laws, then that is acceptable, but spiritually you will have stagnation, no growth, no improvement of the self. In school, you did not remain in nursery for the whole of your school life, each year you progressed up into the next year, you became a junior and eventually a senior student, but you progressed until it was time to leave and attend high school, again you progressed up through the different grades to leaving school. In the spiritual sense, you never leave school or stop progressing, because spiritual progress is unlimited, when you think you have learned all there is to know, there opens up before you more lessons and more knowledge to acquire, but again the desire to learn and progress has to come from within you, for knowledge brings a greater awareness. Wouldn't it be a wonderful benefit to be able to know and understand everything around you, the laws that operate to bring about the happenings around you, knowledge releases you from the darkness of ignorance as does spiritual knowledge launch you into the light of understanding.

Free will is one of the greatest gifts to be bestowed on mankind, if used wisely it can bring unlimited benefit to all, but when used negatively can bring pain and suffering. Do you have the strength to use your gift of free will for the benefit of others? It is very difficult to live your life and not constantly think of yourself, we become sometimes selfish and it is one of life's greatest challenges to put others before ourselves, yes, life is for living and enjoying, but one of the laws of spiritual growth is that the self grows when it is serving others.

WE ARE NOT HERE BY CHANCE

There is a plan for you and me,
We are not here by chance,
You have been placed where you are
For there you will grow best.

It seems as though life's events
Always seek you out,
But spiritual growth does not happen
When life is calm and bright.

When darkness comes into your life,
It's hard to welcome it,
For with it comes a lesson to learn,
You have to handle it.

I never asked for this, you say,
Give this to someone else,
It's far too much for me to bear,
It doesn't make any sense.

You are the only one,
That can handle it this way,
You cannot see the outcome,
Through the clouds on this day.

But know that you will benefit,
Not only you are touched,
By this problem that you want to leave,
And escape its cruel clutch.

Those around you will of course
Support and give you help,
Your struggle and your isolation,
They have also felt.

You have not been alone through this,
We knew that you'd win through,
But everyone involved in this,
Now has a different view.

The lesson has not just been yours,
Though this you couldn't see,
The plan has been fulfilled,
The part you played was the key.

THE SPIRIT OF LOVE

The spirit of love lies within each and every one of you. It seeks expression every day, and it grows and spreads when it is shared with others. There are those who may not accept your loving thoughts or words, but give them anyway. Your kind deeds may be received with disdain, do them anyway, for there your responsibility ends. In giving, you have done your part. You may not see the immediate results of your spiritual work, but know that it has not been wasted or in vain. The smallest task done in love for another, may be reaped you many years hence, because things of the spirit never die. This we know, for our loved ones in spirit, communicate with us time and time again, giving us proof of their survival of physical death and uplifting us with words of love and encouragement. This material life is not all there is, the trials that we endure in this life do not last forever. They are fleeting when compared to the eternity of life but always, our loved ones in spirit stand by our sides, guiding us and giving us the strength to go on. When you struggle and sink to the depths of despair, through that fog of sadness you will eventually see that spot of light. It will just be the size of a pin point at first, but as you focus your attention on it that guiding light of spirit will help you on your ascent back to your path. You had momentarily lost your way, but spirit never left you, they persevered, trying to reach you and never gave up on you until they had achieved their aim.

How many of us have that same determination and persistence of spirit? It is hard for us to go through and experience those hard times, but it is harder still for our loved ones to see us in pain, and to suffer, sometimes as a result of our own actions. They shed tears too, because that bond of love that they had for us when on earth, is now even stronger.

So look for that guiding light, it is there always, and strive to be a guiding light for others, for just as your path is lit by spirit, so you can light the path of another.

15

SURVIVING LIFE'S BATTLES

There comes a time in everyone's life, when one day you just sit down and take stock of your life. You look at all the events that have taken place and how they have brought you to where you are now. There have been moments in your life, when you thought you would not survive, there have been problems that you never thought you would solve, yet you did, for here you are, a survivor, a survivor of many trials.

You sit and you wonder about these events and think, "I wouldn't wish for those things to happen to anyone, yet they happened to me and have made me the person that I am today, I have been moulded by many experiences and none of those experiences were chosen by me".

No my friend, not chosen, but given, and you were never given any experience that you couldn't cope with or problem that you couldn't overcome. Each time you were faced with a new problem, you felt anxious and sometimes fear, but these feelings braced you for a new battle. You drew your strength and did what was necessary to bring yourself out of the other end of the tunnel, but there was always light at the other end of the tunnel, there was always someone there to help carry you to the side and tend your wounds. The gentleman who patted you on the shoulder that day when you were so lonely and sad inside, the lady who smiled at you as though she knew you and lifted your spirit for just that moment, the child that grabbed for your hand as it's mother pushed it past you in it's buggy. You knew none of these people, but spirit had put them to work, inspired them at that moment to let you know that you were not alone, that for now the battle is over and spirit want to embrace and comfort you.

Help is always at hand, and you are always held in the arms of spirit when times are hard, there is always a positive outcome, although this cannot always be seen with the physical eye. It is a great task that our friends in spirit have to fortify and help the lives of all their loved ones here to run smoothly, even when we are in the battle zone their love for us still drives them on to help and guide us as much as they can, without interfering, for they cannot take away our experiences from us, as good or bad as they may seem to be, for we grow spiritually from them, but they constantly pledge to help dry our tears, to soothe that painful heart and shine a light for us in our darkest times.

The love that they show to us we must try and reflect, on those that we know are in need. In the same simple way as the child, with a smile or a pat on the back, the simple gestures can start to warm the coldest of hearts, and bring a smile to someone who has almost forgotten how to.

BE AWARE

Be aware of all that you do, say and think. Be in control at all times, if you cannot achieve these things then strive to make them a reality in your life.

IT IS IN THE TRYING THAT YOUR SPIRIT GROWS, in tenderness and love. In every moment of free time you have, dwell on the spirit that is within you, that seeks to express itself in love. In the quiet moments of your day spirit loved ones draw close to you yearning to let you know that they are with you, wanting to share what they have learned since leaving the earth plane, wanting to share with you the richness of spirit which can be yours now. The love and harmony that they experience daily, they want to experience with you. If you can learn to put the troubles of the physical world to one side momentarily we can reach you, converse with you. Our thoughts can merge with yours and we can impress you with the knowledge and help that you need. We are all one spirit, we are not separate, the love of the creator binds us all together as one. Strive to be humble in your lives, that does not mean to allow others to walk all over you, there is great spiritual strength in humility, in quietude, in stillness, for this is where the strength is acquired. Be positive in your outlook on life, you have heard it said many times that those things of the spirit which are worth having are the hardest to obtain. It is much easier to be negative, you do not have to try very hard to be negative, but a positive attitude is much harder to keep up in the face of negativity, but if you persevere it will become second nature to you.

In time positive attitude will take up residence within you and negative thought will not be able to enter, the spirit of love will eventually embrace you and all who come in contact with you. Be free in your thinking, an open and positive mind knows no restrictions and is open to receive the truth and love from spirit that waits for the opportunity to serve and nurture you. Be understanding of others so that your understanding can grow and encompass universal truths that constantly look for a new host who is willing to share and spread the seeds of truth.

GIVE YOUR LOVE FREELY

In a world that is currently full of strife and negativity, it seems hard sometimes to notice and appreciate the positive vibrations of love that do penetrate the darkness of our world.

The words of love and peace that constantly emanate from our unseen friends and loved ones in spirit, do occasionally, and more often than we think, reach us causing us to be calm and free from fear when we most need it.

Christmas time is no exception, the joy that is normally absent in our daily lives, spreads throughout the land in an ever increasing cloud, building a blanket of positive energy for all to feel and experience. It causes upliftment and smiles, even in the darkest of corners that usually seem untouched by love. Children dance and sing more loudly than usual, parents are more tolerant than usual, surrounding beauties seem to stand out and become more noticeable, the blue sky looks even more blue when the sun shines, for this is the time of year when a cold wind can make you feel a little less amenable towards others, but the overtaking sense of Christmas spirit will melt any feelings of discomfort.

At this time of year, there are many gifts exchanged, but there is one gift from spirit that costs nothing and is given to us freely, it is available to us every day of the year, and it falls into our laps unannounced and without ceremony, and that gift is love. I know you are not surprised by this revelation, for you hear that this is given to you weekly in your services, and as it is given to you so you should also give it freely.

It truly is the only thing that you can give away and become rich, not in earthly riches, but spiritual riches. With each gift you give this Christmas, make sure there is plenty of love wrapped up inside, the gifts you receive this Christmas may not be many in number, but can be spiritually multiplied many times over if the right thoughts are used, do not forget that your thoughts and the motive and reasoning behind those thoughts, affect those that they are directed to.

In thought and deed, send your love and be fruitful, for the gift of love you send today, will undoubtedly be yours in the future.

NEW OPPORTUNITIES

During our lives new doors of opportunity are frequently opened up to us, opportunities to help and serve others, bringing to the fore our own spiritual natures. By helping others selflessly we do ourselves a great credit, for our own spiritual development increases.

One day, when we have left this earthly plain, we will each judge ourselves; this will not be done by another, but by our own self-critical natures. When the material self has fallen away and the true spirit nature of self is revealed, how will we look? Will we shine with the brightness of our earthly deeds, or will that light shine dimly.

In this life you can only steer your own boat, you cannot steer the boat of another. We each have responsibilities that cannot be shared or another blamed for our own actions. If you are unsure about your planned actions then check the motive behind that action. If you are motivated by greed, a need for power, jealousy, hatred, then these actions will have their consequences which each will have to pay.

If your actions are motivated by the desire to help another, then the benefits will be great and pay far better dividends. If the path of spiritual development were an easy one, there would be many souls who were poor in spirit, for very few lessons of spiritual attainment would be learnt. There have been many souls who came before us, who endured much pain in making a smoother path for those who would follow in their footsteps, and we also shall continue to smooth the path for those who may take up the light of spirit and follow. But be steadfast for your steps are guided always, you draw to you those in spirit of like mind and who have the same aspirations. They walk with you through those newly opened doors of opportunity and they keep that light of spirit burning, so that you do not lose your way.

19

I KNEW YOU WERE THERE

As I lay there on my hospital bed,
My life on earth soon to end,
Each day you came and held my hand,
I KNEW YOU WERE THERE.

I felt your warm hand on mine
And your whispered words of days gone by,
Your love and heartfelt thanks for those times,
YES I KNEW YOU WERE THERE.

When you touched my hand to your face
And asked God above not to take
This precious love from this place,
I HEARD YOUR PRAYER.

It seemed as though there was so little time
To express a whole lifetime of love.....and to share
The memories that you held so dear,
I KNEW YOU WERE THERE.

I felt your love get stronger and stronger
As each day past you could no longer
bear to see me get weaker and weaker,
I FELT YOU LET GO.

As loved ones gathered around my bed,
The room fell silent and then became filled
With light which promised to comfort and heal,
I WAS GLAD YOU WERE THERE.

To all who wonder if their loved ones know
That their last days were not spent alone,
Whether in thought or physical presence know,
That LOVE KNOWS NO BOUNDS.

THE SEARCH FOR TRUTH

In this world there are many many different religions, too many to mention. Most people at some time in their lives, embark on the search for spiritual truth, a search that can take you down many roads and avenues, until you find what you feel is truth. There are many religions, but there is only one God, one divine creator, and each religion will say that their God pronounces this or that truth.

God has many attributes and rules for life it seems, when investigating different religions. So how do you find truth? We are all created by that divine creator we call God, every soul was created by Him in love, and each soul incarnated into physical beings at a given time. Every soul knows where it came from, and that knowledge is part of every soul. We all started our lives as a living intelligent energy in the world of spirit.

As physical beings with a soul and a spirit, our search for truth is inevitable, since the soul craves that which takes him closer to home. When information is given to you and called truth, that information cannot be accepted by you if it does not resonate in a positive way with your inner being, it is more than just if the words ring true or not, it is the essence and feeling of that information resonating in harmony with your soul, that determines whether you can accept or reject what you have found in your search.

In this physical life, we have to learn many lessons, the most subtle lessons can pass us by unnoticed and unrecognised, but they will be repeated again and again throughout our physical lifetimes, until we learn and absorb those lessons on a spiritual level, and they become a part of our being. It can take a long time and many hard and harsh situations, before finally understanding, and recognition comes to us.

According to our spiritual and soul development, we will know truth when we see it, so you see, even the many religions that we have in this world, and the different truths that abound, can help us in our search for the truth. We all try many colours in clothing, or otherwise, before we find one that suites us and enhances our good features, making us feel comfortable and good about ourselves. So it is with the search for truth, when you find it, it will enhance your life, and the soul and spirit within will rejoice.

THE LAWS OF SPIRIT

The laws of spirit operate and encompass all, that is, all life in this universe, no matter what form it takes.

We all try to live by a very basic principle of, do unto others as you would have them do unto you, but there are times when we forget this and have momentary lapses of selfishness, and this is understood by our friends in spirit. They do not judge us, as they once walked the same road that we are now walking. They fully understand that we are all human, living in a material world, with all its pressures, and where we daily meet many challenges to our spiritual natures. We meet the challenges and overcome them as best we can, and then we go forward only to meet in time, more difficulties and trials. Most of us get to the stage where we raise our eyes to the heavens and say, "I don't need this, I can't take any more of this constant battering", but surprisingly we do battle through. Each time we find the strength from somewhere deep within, to get over that next hurdle that looms up from seemingly nowhere.

Before incarnating upon this earth, we knew that we would meet many challenges in our physical lifetimes. We were told that we would never be left alone, but through solving our problems we would grow spiritually in strength. Nobody has ever come to this earth and spent a whole lifetime lying on a bed of roses until it was time for their return to spirit. There are physical, spiritual and emotional lessons to learn while we are here, and no matter how well off or easy we judge another's life to be, in comparison with our own, we do not have the capacity to see with the eyes of spirit, to make that judgment.

We judge with a material eye that does not see clearly. We see in terms of the 'haves' and the 'have not's'. From a spirit point of view, the 'haves', who place great value in material gain have turned away from spiritual values, of course this is not always the case, as some are able to achieve a balance between the spiritual and material aspects of life. The 'have not's', often feel they have been dealt a cruel hand in life, but our friends in spirit constantly tell us that material loss is spiritual gain. Your daily challenges are not punishments; their spiritual value is worth far more than any material gold. One day you will see clearly how these challenging situations were akin to the golden threads of spirit, and the tapestry that you created throughout your earthly sojourn is one to be admired and proud of, and nobody will be able to take that from you.

So keep your head up high, there is no battle that cannot be won with the strength of spirit within and behind you.

LIFE'S PROBLEMS

There is nothing in life that you cannot overcome with the help of your loved ones in spirit. There is no problem that is too difficult that spirit will not help you to tackle.

These are bold statements to make, but are truth and can be qualified by a different thought process to that of the norm. In this earth life, overcoming a problem means eradicating it or making it easier to handle, so that it no longer looks like a problem to be dealt with, and there is no longer fear or apprehension there when we look at it. It seems that whenever we have a situation that is not one of normal circumstances, it becomes to us a problem, and on the face of it, it feels and looks troublesome, but the reality is it can teach you something that you wouldn't normally learn in normal situations.

Picking a problem to pieces and analysing every part of it teaches you to use your thought processes in a different and more thorough way, it exercises your physical and your spiritual self, for once feelings get involved with your thinking, your spiritual self becomes active, and this is what is needed in the process of spiritual growth, and each person grows in their own time and space. It cannot be hurried and it has to be paced to the individual's needs and requirements.

You are all guided in this growth process and never left to it alone. Your interest in certain subjects and affairs are used to your advantage in that your problems are taken by you and moulded into such a way that you can compare it to something that you have known and experienced in the past. Each time you look at a problem with feeling, you will use your past experiences to add your knowledge and faith to working towards the outcome and solving your problem.

It gets too technical when you fail to understand the mechanics of problem solving but as long as you invent and keep in your mind a picture of the outcome, you follow that and make it possible to achieve. Your problem is only a problem if you look at it as a whole, but in reality they are many small problems that need to be tackled individually, just like a mosaic picture is made up of small pieces. When the small pieces are put together the final picture is a beautiful combination of colour and shape. If problems are looked at and tackled in this way, you will never be threatened by them, but know that they are not what they seem.

This world also is made up of tiny individuals of shape and colour, and just like a mosaic we are all part of that bigger picture. With spirit's help, you can be the piece that makes the difference and adds to the world's beauty and development towards unity and love.

SPIRITUAL DEAFNESS

Spiritual deafness is suffered by a lot of people. It is caused by wrong teaching and long term beliefs held onto from childhood.

It builds up over a period of time, until the mind becomes completely cut off from any new teachings that we try to inspire. It only takes a moment to switch on that receiver, to allow communication to take place, but there are those who have forgotten where to find that on/off switch. That switch can be found in your heart, for once the realisation comes that your beliefs are not truths, then the process of searching and receiving can begin.

It will vary from person to person in how long and how quickly the process of receiving and accepting spiritual truths take, but according to your spiritual stage of evolution you will receive no more or less than you can cope with and digest at any time.

It is comparative to a sponge, depending on how dry or wet the sponge is, so there is a limit on the amount of water it can soak up. The water is representative of spirit truths and knowledge, the sponge is the mind or your spirit self. It can take many years of earth time for this process to begin and for the spirit to realise that there is a need for taking in this knowledge through earthly experiences, but this is the way you learn, experience is the best teacher, enhanced by knowledge gained from spirit communication.

Knowledge of the physical world is not all there is to know; there are spiritual truths that help to bring harmony to your lives and the physical world, without it the physical world will become a desolate place, devoid of all spiritual light, a desert without an oasis.

People need light to live and the light of spirit seeks to shine even in the darkest of places, the new shoots coming up through the dark soil have laid down firm roots and these roots spread far and wide, even on stony ground.

So take heart, all is not lost, indeed nothing is ever lost once spirit has been introduced to you, the fact is they do not need any introduction, they are with you always, your needs are the only invitation they need, from physical birth to physical death, they await your call, after that there is joyful reunion, when the blind see and the deaf hear, sometimes for the first time.

LOVE IS IN THE AIR

When you are in trouble of any kind, you usually find a telephone number and call for help. If your car breaks down, you will normally, without a second thought, call for physical assistance, which usually arrives after waiting for a short time. This is no different from asking your spirit friends and loved ones for help. We usually forget that this can be done once we are embroiled in our problems.

Our loved ones are just as concerned and caring for us now, as they were when they were here in their physical bodies. We would often phone them and speak to them, telling them of any problems we might be having and feeling better for having shared our difficulties with them, why should it be any different now that you cannot see them. The fact that you can no longer see or hear them, should not change the relationship you had with them and they are certainly still in your life enough, to know what your feelings and problems are at present.

In love they still listen to your thoughts that are sent out into the ether when you are troubled. Do not send your calls for help, with doubt and wonder at whether they can hear you or not. Know that they are with you in every situation good or bad. There are times when your loneliness or situation makes you doubt, you think that if they were with you as you have been told, they would not have let you get into this situation in the first place, that is not the case, your loved ones are not there to prevent you from learning and living your life, or from making free choices, even the Divine Spirit allows you free will to make your choices in life, even if the outcome of that choice and decision seems to be a mistake and is unwanted, but your journey as you travel through life, is yours alone, although you are never alone, and your unwanted situations are not always just for your learning alone. Those around you are also learning and experiencing your situation by observation. We can all quote experiences that other people we know went through, and although their experience was not ours, we were touched and learnt from that situation, in this way we all learn together and can each learn something different according to our own level of understanding.

Our experiences also teach others, so when you are in a situation that feels helpless and out of control, your loved ones are there doing their best to help, but you must ask for help and talk to them with the knowledge that your words are heard and love is in the air, for their love for you never dies.

DON'T GIVE UP

When you feel that you are all alone
And crying tears of pain,
Your life has been turned upside down,
Things just won't be the same.

There doesn't seem to be a day
When things go right for you,
The emotional turmoil that you feel
is very real it's true.

Your whole life seems to have become
A constant battle zone,
With those that you once shared your life,
That love seems to have gone.

But don't give up just yet my dear,
For you are not alone,
There are those unseen by your side
Whose work has now begun.

Your call for help has been heard
As it raises on the ether,
Please be strong and steadfast
For just a little longer.

Your unseen friends are working hard
To clear away the clouds,
That have been blocking out the sun,
That once shone without bounds.

The day will come when you'll look back
And see that those dark days
Were necessary to endure,
Just a passing phase.

In life there'll always be
A storm that seems will not let up,
But the heavier the storm, the brighter the sun will shine,
Pleas don't give up.

A new day is dawning and soon you will see
That you were never alone,
Each time you fell, we helped you up,
You found strength to carry on.

Good times come with hard times,
They're not always easy to bear,
But rest assured and know,
That when you call, we will be there.

One day you will be helping someone else
Through what you've suffered,
You'll know exactly what to say,
Your support you will have offered.

Then you will know
Just why you had to go through what you did,
In life all our experiences are lessons
And never wasted.

YOUR SPIRITUAL SELF

Be aware of your spiritual self. You are spirit here and now and you will continue to be spirit when the physical overcoat that you wear throughout this life, falls away and becomes dust. Your life will continue for an eternity, for there is no death.

Spirit cannot die, it can only grow stronger, absorbing and learning from new experiences. Ashes to ashes, dust to dust, then add to that, freedom. The release from the physical body is like that of a bird released from its cage, it is not a moment to fear, but a time of liberation from chains that held fast. Most of you will have experienced the feeling of loss, when one loved dearly makes that short journey from the earth to spirit. Know that they did not make that journey alone. In physical life you all have your spirit companion, who is with you from birth, through every life challenge, through all your sorrows, good times and bad. There are also loved ones, of family and friends who went before you, whose ties of love to you have never been broken. Would they now desert you in your greatest hour of need? No, they move ever closer, for in that moment of physical release, hands outstretched in loving embrace, they will accompany you to your new home, which you are even now building for yourselves.

There is rest for the weary, and then joyful reunion with loved ones who have waited patiently for your arrival. You slowly grow accustomed to your new surroundings in increasing wonder at the beauty that touches and enthrals your senses. Then your mind becomes aware of the loved ones left behind on earth. You begin to feel, through that bond of love, the emotions of your friends and relatives, the sadness and the tears. They mourn for you and you feel their loss and pain, "Do not cry for me", you tell them, but they are deaf to your pleas, and numb to your touch, you want them all to know that you are now more alive than you have ever been. In their quiet moments you try to communicate your presence, sometimes, just occasionally, you will think you saw your loved one look at you, for a second there, you are sure they saw you, they must have for now their mind is replaying memories of your time together, loving memories, the tears begin to flow, you kiss your loved one on the cheek, and immediately they touch their face, there, your first communication, it was worth every effort. They know that death can never separate you, the bond of love can never be broken, there truly is no sting in death, for love is the great comforter, and life is eternal.

A RAY OF LIGHT THROUGH PARTING CLOUDS

When all seems lost and futile, and you feel that you have come to the end of the road, without another road to take in sight, there comes to you an unexplainable calm. It is a calm and a stillness that we usually describe as a feeling of numbness, of not being able to feel any emotion and being devoid of all awareness of what is happening around and about us.

This is the time and the place when spirit does most of their work with us. This is the time, when we put up the least barriers and allow spirit to enter our lives and help, for when you have sunk as low as you think you can, there is only one way that you can go, and that is up.

In the worst times of our lives, comes the help that you cry for, the seeming dark clouds begin to part and there you begin to see the smallest ray of light forcing its way through the now parting clouds. Our loved ones watch and see all that goes on, they see and feel our emotions and so do not always need an invitation to help. Our thoughts and feelings of despair speak a thousand words and do not always have to be verbalised.

There are too many times when we think that we are alone in our troubles, but this is not so, we receive help even when we haven't asked, for the influence of our loved ones in spirit is always for a positive end and outcome. They want us to live happy and fulfilling lives and once that bond of love is there between us, it continues beyond the grave and the funeral of sadness. They shine that light of love and hope wherever and whenever they can in our lives, and want you to know that. There may be those in spirit now that did not show their kindness when on earth for many earthly reasons, but for most the doorway of death brought to them enlightenment and spiritual truth that they were unaware of when in the physical body.

When the veil fell from their eyes on entering the spirit life, the truth was clear, and their now spirit eyes could not deny what they could now see. There is spiritual progress open to all who desire to seek it, both here in the physical world and in the spirit realms, for those who wish to remain spiritually stagnant, they will have their wish until such time as their thinking becomes different, but for those whose minds seek for higher and further understandings, help and assistance is always given in abundance.

For the seeker of spiritual light, there is adventure and knowledge in never ending quantities, for there is no end to the knowledge that is available. Spiritual growth is the only true way to acquire truth, and once you have that, the wings of truth will set you free

LIFE'S EXPERIENCES

Living this life is not as simple and problem free as we would like it to be. It is and always will be, a life of sometimes emotional pain and also moments of pleasure, always a mixture, like a mixed bag of sweets, soft, hard and chewy, but doesn't that add to the excitement of life?

A bag of sweets all the same colour, taste and consistency will get pretty boring after a while, and you'll just want to give them away. In order to get the most out of life that you can, apply yourself in the best way and to the best of your ability. We all need to know and understand what it is like to experience all these different emotions that we can feel in just a 24-hour period. It makes more sense to us when we have experienced and felt the same emotions that another is going through. How can you say, "I understand how you feel", when you have not experienced another's feelings, how can you say, "I know and understand what you are going through".

There are a wide range of emotions, that throughout our lifetime we will feel, experience and know, and they are to us, sometimes negative, positive and uplifting, but in order to gain the experience, you have to go through the gamut of different situations, to increase your knowledge and make you worthy of the words, 'experienced' and 'trustworthy'.

In any application for a new job, you are asked about your experience, for without that experience, you may find great difficulty accomplishing the work, which you are being asked to do. With that experience, you become a trusted member of that work force. In life, it is the same principle, your experiences, spiritual and physical, emotional and mental, will be the deciding factors upon whether you are a worthy mentor for another, who is in need of your help and encouragement.

In life, we all need each other, for no man is an island, but if you treat each situation that you enter into as, 'my next lesson in life', and allow each new situation to teach you something, then you will not be so fearful. We are all here to learn, and each new day brings us fresh new lessons, do not fear them, for in time, you will be able to teach another the same lessons, with gentleness, experience and knowledge, easing their pathway in the way you would have liked yours to be.

Take and use your knowledge of spirit with you as a lamp light during your life's lessons, for they may seem daunting at first, but as your eyes grow accustomed to the dim light of your new adventure, the light of spiritual knowledge will brighten your path, until your eyes see without any strain at all.

CHANGE STARTS WITH YOU

Is today the right day for you to make changes in your life? You may have for a long time, been wishing that things around you and in your life, were different. Changes seem to happen all around us constantly, the weather changes, the seasons change, sometimes quite suddenly, but usually gradually.

As with the seasons, there is a certain time set for the changes that take place, but only when certain criteria are set in place, can these changes happen.

In our lives, we live each day in the best way that we can, sometimes our lives become very predictable and monotonous, and we yearn for something different, for something to take us out of the rut we seem to be in, we wish for new experiences and new people to enter our lives, we may even wish for people to vacate our lives, depending on our present circumstances and experiences.

What if tomorrow you could wake up and everything could be different, what would you have to do to make those changes within yourself before external changes begin to take place? Could it be that a change in your thinking has to take place first, before those changes in your life can actually take place? Supposing the events that are taking place in your life and the immediate environment are actually a mirror image of yourself. Do you need to be more positive in your outlook, in order to have that peace that you constantly search for?

There is only one way to find out, the changes that you want to make in your life, have to start from the inner self. If you want order and peace and serenity in your life, try and become all these things, embrace love, embrace tolerance, embrace happiness and peaceful things, so that you become immersed in them, become the cause and you will experience the effect, for life is truly what you make it, and your thoughts affect everything you do, they affect everyone you meet, for they are you.

Take control of your life by taking control of your thoughts, one of the hardest things to do, since most of us spend our lives being dominated by our thoughts. We are always surrounded by thoughts, and the results of someone else's thoughts. This building and everything in it began as a thought. Use your thoughts lovingly and positively, for a positive spirit will always triumph the trials of life helping you to achieve that which your heart desires.

LIGHT MY PATH

I pray for all my soul's desires,
I pray that I may love you,
That all my thoughts will be of truth,
And desires that bring me to you.

If love is truly the only way,
That I can make true progress,
Then open my heart and eyes that I,
May follow the path of goodness.

Please show me the light along this path,
I verily need to follow,
For when darkness comes to blur my sight,
I will need you in my sorrow.

This path I take may not be fixed,
Many detours I will make,
But show me signs along the way,
To get me back on track.

Be ever near me Lord I pray,
For I am but a child,
I ask in earnest for your love,
To make me meek and mild.

Your strength and love I yearn for,
When in stress and times of need,
I come in all humility,
For truth and light to receive.

EXPRESSING SPIRITUAL VALUES

It is very hard to live in a material world with all our physical shortcomings, and at the same time, try to express spiritual values, for the two seem to be in direct opposition.

To express love and understanding when all around you is constant negativity, sometimes makes you think, well why should I bother, what difference will it make to anybody, people don't want to hear that love can heal, people don't want to try to be tolerant of another who is abusive in the way that they conduct themselves, why should just one person make all that effort for it to fall on seemingly deaf ears. No positive action or word is ever wasted, it may seem that spiritual thoughts, actions and deeds done for another, become or seem to be a waste of effort, but they are not. They find their home, if they are not accepted by the one they are directed at, it means they are not ready. Spiritual growth is individual, the pace is different for all, if you were all at the same stage of spiritual growth, then the spirit world would be able to convert everyone on mass, a mass conversion of every soul to love and light, that of course our world is in need of, but it cannot work that way.

We are like the grains of sand on a beach, each grain holds within it energy, energy which grows with the daily toil of life, but within that energy is the light of spirit, which seeks to express itself, but is limited in its expression by the stage of evolution that has been reached. It causes the inner spirit much frustration at not being able to give full expression of itself, but as we evolve and grow, both physically and spiritually, the light of spirit will spread, the love will permeate even the hardest of physical shells, and you will be able to walk without fear, along the beach of your life, breathing in the uplifting energy that is yours by right, feeling the sun on your back, and the richness of the earth beneath your feet, it is all yours to take, but are you ready?

Spiritual truth and knowledge is free, when you are ready to receive it, it will find its way to you in many different ways, and in a way you find welcoming and acceptable. The caterpillar cannot turn into a butterfly before it is ready, and so with knowledge, the soil has to be rich in nutrients to receive the seeds in order for them to grow to an eventual harvest. If the soil is not ready there will be no growth, therefore prepare yourselves for the receipt of spiritual truths and knowledge so that one day your harvest will be full and wholesome and can be shared with all who are in need.

Let your faith keep you and guide you, for the sunshine of spirit never fails to uplift the weary.

THE DIVINE SPIRIT GIVES FREELY

The love and gentleness of the Divine Spirit surrounds and interpenetrates every part of your being. The Divine Spirit who has many names but only one purpose is round and about you always. Your ability to be aware of His closeness is increased when you withdraw into the silence, His presence then becomes more apparent. You see daily around you, manifestations of His beauty, His law and His gifts to you in nature. None can surpass this intelligence which created the universe and all that is expressed within it. There is nothing to add and nothing to take away to make its beauty become more than it already is.

We, mankind, are the temporary holders of the deeds to this world that we live in, it has been given to us in trust, and this privilege we should not misuse. It helps us to know that the beauty in nature thrives year after year without any real thought from us, but that when it sleeps through the quiet and regenerative seasons it will burst forth again in all its glory, showing its power and strength even in the most adverse conditions, for it was created to express and to give, sharing all that it has. Mankind with all his intelligence has not yet learnt this lesson, that to give and to share with his neighbour is the only way to fulfilment and happiness. We still isolate ourselves from each other, believing that what each has should be kept. There are countries that live in poverty, kept down by their rich leaders, who keep for themselves, never learning that the population that they rule would have a lot to give in return for their increased bread, for the bread of life increases when nurtured and watered with love.

The Divine Spirit gives freely, without the need for repayment, He gives in abundance that which we need, the air we breathe, the richness of the soil, the sunshine and the rain, the bread and the breath of life. In return we grow, spiritually, so that the next generation will grow, harnessing all the knowledge that we have to give and growing still further. It is all that we have to give that ensures the vitality and the nurturing carries on, from generation to generation.

Take all the knowledge that you have been given, process it and use if for the benefit of your brother and sister, for they will carry that knowledge to the farthest of lands. In your daily toil of life, gently pass on your knowledge of spirit, so that eventually the love of the Divine will flower and grow and be spread around the earth, for once you have knowledge you have personal responsibility. Give freely so that when you receive, it will be in abundance and that abundance you will want to share, for within you all is the spirit which seeks to give and receive love.

We are always being told that our loved ones in spirit are close to us, and that they never leave us in times of trouble, or when we are experiencing pain, both emotionally and physically, but what does that mean?

Does it mean they are close to us physically, or does it mean they are close in thought? It means both, there is no distance between this physical world and the spirit world, that is, no distance in miles, thought is sent and received as quickly as the thought can be formed in your mind. How quickly does the thought to pick something up from the floor, take for the thought to form in your mind, through to the actual action taking place? How quickly does the thought of lifting one foot up off the floor take from the thought form, to the action of actually doing it, it takes seconds for a fully formed thought to reach it's destination.

The world is kept going by many thoughts, most are good thoughts, some are not so good. We communicate by thought, and so it is with our loved ones, their thoughts of love and best wishes are sent to us continuously. We need to look beyond this material world with all its material trappings and seek the spiritual world and its many truths by listening to the thoughts that our loved ones communicate to us all the time. Do not forget that we are all spirit, with minds of spirit, for one day, we will all shed these physical bodies and leave them behind, but even while still inhabiting the physical body we are still able to rise above the material and the physical problems of this earth by the use of thought, spirit is king and the body is the servant, not the other way around.

In this life that we live, we have choices and we make many in our lifetime on earth, but if you decide to serve matter instead of the spirit, then the law of cause and effect, will swing into action, for it is an unchangeable law put into place by the Divine Spirit and shows no favouritism.

The spirit within is eternal, and has an eternity to learn, but what you learn must be put into practice, for to know the truth of spiritual laws, and pretend that you do not know, living your life contrary to those laws, will cause you to reap the seeds that you have sown. In your heart is a key, put there by the Divine Spirit. That key is love, it is within us all in varying measures, if you can be true to your spirit and the Divine Spirit, that key will unlock for you many gifts, both in this world and the next.

So open your hearts and let the wisdom of spirit in, for in that wisdom, you will find many treasures.

CHRISTMAS ESSENCE

At this time of year, in the run up to Christmas day, there emerges a spiritual feeling of well-being, which seems to spread across the world, and then on Christmas day there is a sudden surge of love and tolerance and unconditional giving. The whole world suddenly seems to care; people begin to think about the feelings of others. We begin also, to send out our thoughts to our loved ones in spirit, who made their transition to their new homes at around this time.

Love is being sent and exchanged all over the globe. What a wonderful thought to be able to live in this atmosphere daily. What a change would come to the world, if it could last for more than the few days of Christmas, for these are the spiritual values that our loved ones try to teach us to live by, for all the other 11 months of the year. You do not have to use Christmas day as an excuse for shaking the hand of a stranger, or for giving a spontaneous smile. This spiritual cloud that seems to have enveloped the earth at this time can truly be put to good use, any day, any time, at any hour. It matters not what your religion, nor your status or standing in life, for we are all one spirit, and sharing and giving of yourself is the true essence of love, and this naturally draws spirit to us.

Those who are seemingly alone at this time, also have many friends in spirit, who draw ever closer to them, trying hard to let them know that they do not walk alone, and again their love surrounds them, but is a loving thought sent out enough, you ask? Love given unconditionally and with heartfelt feeling, can change every negative to a positive, for thought sent forth, with love behind it, can never fail to meet its target, the changes may not be immediate, but it is enough to set those changes in motion. When you are in distress and you call on spirit for help, the emotion behind that call ensures that your loved ones receive that call loud and clear. If a request for help is made for another, with the same feeling and emotion, how much more likely is it to be heard, for the very act of selflessly thinking of others, brings the love of spirit to your door, for they love you without the need for that love to be returned, and so when you demonstrate that same love, its strength and measure you cannot truly know, for to measure things of the spirit you cannot use a physical yardstick.

Let us all help to make the essence of Christmas day, a part of every day living, and together we can change the world.

THOUGHTS OF LOVE

Every day, those who we still love, and whose bond of love is never broken because they are now in spirit, watch our daily struggles in this earthly life, still wanting to be a part of our lives as much as they can, still having hopes and best wishes for us in the good times and the bad.

They still attend our celebrations and festivities as part of the family circle, and why should that change, they are still alive and well, having left this physical world with all it's material trappings, and life now continues for them in a spirit world where reality and the truth of life is experienced in every way.

It is a world, we are told, where life is experienced with a heightened sense of being alive, for without the body of clay, which belongs to this physical world, the senses are set free to sense and feel in a way that was not possible while in the physical body. But is that world so far removed from this one, or do we think it is so, and so it is? Is the spirit world and the physical earth world so far apart that one is up and the other down? There is no distance of miles between the two worlds; there is only the distance of thought.

In the distance and the time that a thought can travel, your loved ones can be here, and in a thought's time, you can speak and communicate with them when you are wondering how they are, or needing their love at a difficult time. There is an intermingling of the two worlds, they co-exist. Physicists will tell you that there is no such thing as empty space, the whole universe is living and pulsating with life. There is never a time when those who have left this earthly plane, have withdrawn their love from us. If there was a bond of love when they were here, upon the death of the physical body, that bond of love strengthens, until spirit meets spirit. It is never too late to send a thought of love to the one you called friend.

It is always the right time to send those same thoughts of love to those in need on the earth plane, for in the same way that your thoughts reach those in spirit, distance does not prevent those thoughts reaching those experiencing troubled times here. Send your love on the wing of a thought; you will undoubtedly experience that boomerang effect, where it comes back to you in many ways. Use the key which the Divine Spirit has given you, it is kept in your heart and it can be used at any time. Love, conquers all.

SELF CONTROL

In the midst of all your turmoil and strife that you may be experiencing, there is always help available to you.

In your darkest moments know that you are not alone. Physical life is not a bed of roses for any of us; we have many struggles to contend with, just to get by and through each day. We have to make decisions that we know will affect those around us.

Life is a merry-go-round of many emotions, but we all have to learn control, to not let our emotions erupt and get out of control, we have to learn that our emotions, out of control, can be damaging. The control that you learn to use today and in this life, will hold you in good stead for the future, for one who dominates his emotions effectively, will be seen as wise and in tune with his surroundings and others. You have to remember that you are spirit first and physical body second, for one is eternal and the other perishable, returning at the end of physical life, to the elements.

The spirit does not know all there is to know, but continues to learn even after the death of the physical body, and during this earthly life, will learn and express it's abilities, even though they are sometimes hidden and in need of an awakening to it's innate truths. The same truths that you learn here are the same truths that you will learn in the world of spirit, only in the world of spirit you will have the ability to learn things that could not be learnt while in the physical body, as they will be truths pertaining to the spirit realms.

In this life, too often our emotions spill over and we say and do things we would not normally do and say in a calmer state of mind, there is an element of lashing out with the tongue, and sometimes physically. In error we do these things, and sorrow for what is done engulfs us, but there is a way of preventing this erupting emotion from beginning its journey upwards and outwards. The person you direct that negative emotion to, is a spirit loved by the Divine Father just like you. Many of you have told your own children, not to fight or argue, because he or she is your sister or brother who is entitled to have a different opinion and to think differently. He or she is allowed to live and function in their way, whether you agree with it or not, providing they do you no harm. How much more then must the creator feel about this same cause of wars and unsettlement amongst His children.

In life, we all try to live by what we feel is right or wrong. There is a time for all kinds of emotion, but the negative emotions do not reap positive ends. Understanding another's feelings and emotions is not easy but making an effort and trying to hold a little love in the heart for another, will go a long way to easing even the most fragile of circumstances.

Making that little bit of effort, can go a long way, whether you are thanked for it or not, for even if they do not know the effort that you made, there are higher forces that helped you, and know how hard you tried. Before acting, ask for help and guidance from your spirit friends and helpers, your appeal for help will always be heard and acted upon with love and grace.

PERSONAL RESPONSIBILITY

You are personally responsible for what you do and what you think, because what you do and think affects other people and ultimately will affect you. First and foremost we are all spirit, that is a spirit within a physical body. If you will accept that as a truth then you will realise that we are all one as a people, since we all originate from the same source of that greater spirit. The physical clothing or body that you wear while here on earth is of little significance compared to the reason for your being here and the lessons that you have to learn. Your physical body is just a vehicle or house for your spirit. Yes you have to nurture and care for your physical body in order to have a perfect vehicle through which your spirit can best express itself. While here, your spirit seeks to learn and experience different lessons. In every situation that you experience your spirit will absorb the essence of that situation. The spiritual lessons learnt from the outcome of a whole lifetime of experiences will help you in that future life to come. Our loved ones return to us time and time again offering help and advice in our difficult times. They use their lifetime experiences, coupled with their knowledge of the operation of spirit laws, which they now see clearly, to help us with our daily lives. They have learnt the importance of harmonious living and now understand the laws of cause and effect. If in the course of your life, spiritual harmony is disrupted then the effect will be physical disharmony. It is not always the case that another has caused your physical problems. Learn always to look to yourself first for the answer. Did you do, say or think something to cause this effect? Is your spirituality in harmony with that of those around you, these issues of self should be addressed first. If you can be spiritually at peace with yourself then those around you will instinctively seek to keep that peace. Look to the spiritual in all that you do and love will automatically follow.

LIFE'S DREAM

One day I woke up from a dream,
It seemed so very real,
I lived in a place where people
Were not always what they seemed.

Most people that I met were kind
And generally sincere,
We helped each other when we could
And problems we would share.

But there were those who would not
Find it in their hearts to help
Another who was suffering
In need or down on luck.

Things were very hard sometimes
And I would often cry,
I'd bow my head into my hands
And ask the question why?

I'd often feel like I had nothing
And others had it all,
Life did not seem fair to me
With my back against the wall.

At other times the clouds would lift
And the sun shone in my life,
At times like this I have to say
I felt glad to be alive.

I often found it difficult
To tolerate another
Who did not think or look like me,
Though I knew he was my brother.

Please tell my why I had this dream
And why I acted so,
I cannot see the reason why,
But you must surely know.

My child, your dream was your whole life
Lived on the earthly plain,
Your experiences were those of which
We have all had to obtain.

The hard times were a challenge
For your spirit which has grown
In strength and beauty and is now
Worthy to wear the crown.

The good times were the gifts of spirit
From whom you got your strength,
We never left you all alone,
Especially when you wept.

But don't look back and wish
That you had done things differently
You have plenty of time to learn,
You have all eternity.

A LINK OF LOVE THROUGH PRAYER

In a crowd you can feel all alone, for loneliness visits us all at times. It is at these times when these feelings of doubt arise, and passion for something new to come into your life is experienced, that the light of spirit descends upon us.

There is never any need for feeling alone, once you have the knowledge of spirit's existence and love for us. There is only one way to get through these difficult times, and that is to have faith in those you love in the world of spirit, that they will come to you in your times of need and guide you through this rough patch, this cloud that you are passing through is only temporary. You are being led by the hand and guided to the shores of rest and recuperation, for sometimes the troubled mind can be tried and seemingly beaten, until the will to get over the troubled times is weak, but do not doubt that your helpers and friends in spirit are with you, they lift your feet one at a time to aid each step that you take. They are indeed your angels of mercy, and always at the right time.

You have seen them and felt them around you, a faint breeze against your cheek, when spirit hands have sought to console you, the very hint of an aroma, beautiful and lifting to the senses, a slight movement of your hair when no one is around you, a light touch of the shoulder, these are but a few of the signs that are given to us at times when we are feeling low in mood.

But let us not forget, that a prayer from the heart to the creator of all is still one of the most powerful ways of creating that link between the world of spirit and the mortal residing on the earth plane. That link of love, through prayer, will remain a cast iron one, never to be broken until that inevitable reunion which comes to us all in time. In the meantime, the love that we share with those in spirit continues back and forth across the bridge that we have built with our now unseen friends, but felt very strongly in our times of need.

You no longer need to make a wish for help, wishful thinking is not required, a strong positive thought sent out is enough to attract the help you need, a warm embracing hug will soon be felt by you, as the reassuring sun comes at last from behind that cloud of doubt and loneliness, and once again all is well in your life, but be mindful to give thanks for the good times in your life, for they are a gift and remember that behind every dark cloud there is sunshine, waiting for the opportunity to shine.

CHRISTMAS SPIRIT

Christmas is approaching, which is a time we have been taught, is for giving. What exactly are we giving at this time? I know we tend to give each other lots of gifts, material gifts. We go over our bank balances and spend way too much, because we must be giving. Are we giving spiritually? Are we picking up the phone and calling those we know will be feeling very alone at this time? Are we thinking and feeling with our hearts, love for the many orphans that have been made through war this Christmas, or are we purely just thinking, "Right, what can I buy next?"

You see, spirit have a way of making us think without the materialistic hats that we usually wear. This is, and should be a time of spiritual understanding, and in its own way, a growing and blooming of the soul. It is without doubt, a time when the world is coming together with one mind for a spiritual séance and worshipping of spiritual values.

The heart is about to open and receive the love that is shed by our Divine Father, and in turn, we are going to take that love and share it equally amongst our loved ones. The heart is ready and willing to embrace the purity of spirit and lay aside the dense and heavy form of materialism.

As the world comes together on Christmas day, take a moment, when you open your eyes that morning, to give thanks for all that you have at that time, remember that the world is still in its infancy, compared to how it will be in hundreds of years from now, and in the same way, we are also in the nursery of our lives compared to the spiritual growth we will achieve, in that future of eternity. This is an opportunity for each one of us to grow in spirit, by making that commitment to spirit.

In this material world that we live in, there also lives with us, side by side the higher form of love that we can access at any time, through our prayers and our deeds, we can achieve that oneness of spirit that forms and shapes this world. In every part of this world, there is a design, which has a blueprint, a master plan, which has already been laid down, and the foundations of love have already started to be built upon. This Christmas, let each of us add to those foundations another brick of charity, love and understanding of spiritual values that keep our soul and spirit on a higher vibration of growth and aspiration.

Let the spirit of Christmas and all it truly represents; enter your heart and your home.

NEW BEGINNINGS

A new year has begun, and some of us will have begun the New Year by setting ourselves New Year resolutions, and some of us will have already broken them.

It is a time when we hope for positive changes to enter our lives, and we resolve to put into action new rules that we set for ourselves, in order to achieve those changes.

What resolutions do you think spirit would like us to make? For they are with us daily, encouraging us and helping us to live our lives in the best way that we can. We need to make resolutions that are not so far out of reach, that they are impossible to achieve. It should quite rightly be a time for new beginnings as, for the world, it is sorely needed.

Common courtesy is one resolution that we could all make, it is simple enough and achievable, a great place to start and to put into practice. You see if the world is to change for the better, we have to begin with the individual, ourselves. We are all a small part of the whole, the whole picture, the big wheel of life, spirit. We have to work from within. It is no use praying and wishing for peace to come to the world, and expecting it to happen without each individual playing their part, small as it may seem to be, it matters.

If you start with self, the inner self, that peace will come, it will work its way outwards and manifest into a positive force for the world. The chair that you now sit on was once just a thought, an idea, but now they are in every home and building throughout the world, there is your proof that thoughts of love and peace can one day manifest as a tangible force that can be felt by all. It is not such a difficult resolution to achieve. You naturally want to help those that are troubled, those that are sick, and those that are starving, sometimes through the hand of their leaders, but maybe it is time for the leaders to be shown how to lead, by their followers setting the example, to lead by example and show that only love and tolerance and sharing what you have is the only acceptable way forward, and the lamb can lay beside the lion in harmony, for even they are a part of the wheel of life that we are all a part of.

Look within yourselves for the answers to the questions on world peace, start with peace in your home, for that is where your heart is. It is not an unachievable goal, it is your birthright, and should begin with you. Resolve to become a leader for peace today, today in your home, tomorrow the world.

May peace and love reign for you in this new year.

GIVE THANKS

Many times in our lives we will fall down and pick ourselves up again, we will find ourselves in situations where we are feeling as though nothing is going right for us, and the days will seem long and dark. We will search for the answers to our problems, and it will sometimes seem as though the answers are denied us, but this is not so. We are all, in our life's journey going to occasionally come up against a brick wall, stubborn and unrelenting, but that wall always has a door in it that you haven't yet found. The wall may be tall and wide, and no matter how far along that wall you may walk, you cannot seem to find a way out, and no matter how high you jump, you cannot see over it. But one day, unexpectedly, you look at that wall, the same wall you have been looking at day after day, and suddenly you see a chink of light coming through a door that wasn't there before, and on your side of the door there is no handle, how could it possibly have suddenly appeared and been opened? You push the door open and walk through, out of the darkness into the light. As you turn to close the door on the bitter experience that you have just come through, you see that there is a door handle on this side of the door, there seems to be no one else around to give thanks to, but you see often the door out of your despair is opened by someone on the other side, your calls and shouts for help are always heard, and even when you cannot see who opened the door for you, give them your thanks, for the hand of your spirit friends and loved ones is never far away, and is usually on your shoulder giving comfort and healing in your times of need.

Look back over the years of your life and you will see many times when the hand of spirit opened doors for you, and guided you onto a new pathway in your life. You will have taken many different pathways in your life to get to where you are at present. If you like where you are in your life now and are happy, realise that you could not have got there alone. If your situation at the moment is unsettled and not to your liking, know that there are more doors that have not yet been opened for you, but undoubtedly will be at the right time, for at the end of every pathway of experience is a new door to be opened, and spirit often have the key, but you must knock and wait patiently, for a new pathway entered upon too soon will see you unprepared and could prove to be long and laborious, but with the strength of prior experience and knowledge your new pathway will be eased and benefit you and those around you.

THERE'S MORE TO YOU THAN MEETS THE EYE

One day in eternity's future, you will be forgiven all the wrongs that you have done to another, and you also will forgive all those that you feel have wronged you. For in the world of spirit, where your loved ones who have gone before you now live, feelings of ill will towards another, are not held on to. There is only love and understanding of actions carried out while here on the earth plane, and of course the law of cause and effect will naturally come into play. But feelings of anger and hurt, eventually dissipate and are replaced by feelings of knowing, and understanding how and why thoughts behind a person's actions took place. Clarity of vision will help and enable you to see the whole instead of just a very small part of a person and a situation.

While in the physical body, we are not able to see beyond what is physically presented to us, occasionally we get a glimpse of what is behind the physical aspects of life, and it can elevate us spiritually for a moment or two, but it does not seem to last, and our limited vision is again resumed. Sometimes with great effort, we try to see through the dark glasses of physical sight, and we must continue to make that effort. That saying that we use, "there's more to you than meets the eye", is true and is true for everyone that we meet along the path of physical life, there is a lot more to me and you than just the body of flesh. We are all spirit within this physical shell, that is what survives physical death, and that is what we must try to communicate with in others as well as ourselves.

Spirit communication is not just about communicating with those that are no longer within a physical body, that is just a small part of our search for spiritual knowledge, but we tend to forget that the spirit within is in need of expression, it also needs your attention. It remains latent within if neglected and not activated, for it is an essential part of you that is waiting to work, waiting to be put to good and positive use. It loves the challenge in life, when once overcome, it can shine that little bit brighter, for the spirit within shines at its brightest when life's battles present, for therein we find our strength, "I don't know how I got through that situation", we've all said at one time or another, the strength within, that our spirit provides as a well of strength to constantly draw from, is where we get that strength, and it keeps us away from the precipice, that's the strength of our own spiritual selves.

Get to know your true spirit, you don't yet know what you are capable of , bring that spirit within forth and let it shine as a beacon for others, for in so doing you will help to light the path for one who is in need of spiritual strength and sustenance.

46

CREATE YOUR FUTURE NOW

During this life's journey, we will make many mistakes and be misunderstood due to things we do and say. We may leave this earth plane with many regrets about things we did not do and should have done, but at the point of physical death, all these things in the way of memories will leave us until we enter the world of spirit.

After a short while, our memories of our earth life will return, and we will realise that the life we have lived in the physical body was only for a short time, in comparison to the eternal life we now have ahead of us. What impact will your earthly life have upon your spirit, will your memory of your life be a pleasant one? or will it cause you pain to remember? Did you live your life according to spiritual values that you had been taught or did you just live your life ignoring the fact that you create your future by your acts and deeds of today. Personal responsibility is very real and is truly personal, for the sowing of every seed shall be reaped personally. The sea of life is one which we all sail upon, and we all steer our own ships, rough seas can evoke different reactions from each of us, but the wheel is yours and yours alone to steer, the sea that we sail upon today will eventually lead to the larger oceans of our future, a future that stretches much further than our eyes can see, and yet there is an anchor that we can use at any time, to just stop and get your breath and take stock of the events that are taking place in your life.

For a moment you can drop anchor and meditate on the fact that you are spirit now and forever more, and by withdrawing into the silence for just a moment you will be shown that guiding lighthouse that you so desperately need to see in the darkness of difficulty in your life, if you keep your eye firmly fixed on that light, you will steer your boat around the rocks and eventually into the calmer waters.

For each and every one of us there is always calm after the storm, it is the natural course of life, just as spring follows winter. If you were able to glimpse your future and didn't like what you saw, you would immediately start making changes in your life to ensure that that type of future for you did not come about.

Start creating your future now, make the effort now, there are not many things that we can be sure of in life, but one thing we do know for sure is that we will all eventually return to spirit, taking with us our memories of the life we have lived, in full colour and detail. Today you can make your future as bright and harmonious as you want it to be, by using the love that is within you to help others and ultimately help yourself spiritually.

47

HEAVENLY LOVE

Come with me to a place,
Where I will show you true love,
A place where it enfolds you,
In a way that you should know.

It seeps into your very soul,
Your heart does not escape,
This love is pure and all knowing,
It's yours for you to take.

A calmness and a happiness,
That you could never imagine,
In your world it is but a shadow,
But here we call it heaven.

You do not have to work too hard
To receive or gain this love,
It comes to all who seek its power,
It comes to you through prayer.

Before you close your eyes at night
And reflect upon your day,
Ask Him that what tomorrow will bring,
Is, Your Love I Pray.

THERE IS A PLAN

This earthly life only lasts for a short while, in view of eternity, even 100 years is a short time. You must consider that when you come to this earth plane, you have a plan, a plan that is individual and personal to you. It is a path that you have chosen to walk while you are here, and wise ones in spirit, whom you may or may not know during your physical life, guide you on your path, helping you to achieve your plan.

It matters not that you sometimes feel that you have failed, for opportunities arise time and again' for you to fulfil your destined work. When you feel comfortable with what you are doing, know that you are following your planned path. When feelings of discomfort and agitation take a hold, you will know that change is about to unfold in your life, but there is never any need for fear at this time, for change can mean another step up the ladder of spiritual growth for you.

The work you do while you are here are lessons and experiences that you need to go through, for that is how the spirit within grows and life's experiences are the best teacher. Is it any wonder that we are afraid to walk into new situations, when you think of the myriad of lessons that we have had to learn up to now. It seems sometimes to get harder and harder, but in reality, each experience prepares us for the next. Our loved ones in spirit know of our fears and anxieties, but they always give us that extra little push, encouraging us to take the next step, cushioning us from blows that some time ago, may have floored us. We need never fear that they may not be with us for when we need them most they surround us with their love and strengthen us with their gentle words of encouragement. You do hear them, for when you think or say, "that situation reminded me of the time when a similar thing happened to so and so, who is now in spirit". And you thought you were alone? How many times have you said something and thought afterwards, I sounded just like my mum/dad when I said that. Their loving influences are closer than you think. Eternal love from your loved ones includes now, they are never very far away from you.

The future stretches a long way in front of you, there is no need for fear, in any capacity, for opportunities will continue to appear along your life's path to ensure that you grasp missed opportunities, put right what you feel you did wrong last time, and give you the lessons that you need for spiritual growth and awareness.

The future is yours, just enjoy the journey and let the light of spirit be your guide.

A LETTER FROM SPIRIT

Dear loved one,

I am writing to you from the world of spirit, a world that is bright and full of beauties that mere words would not be able to convey the fullness of.

It is a world where love rules supreme and darkness of thought or deed cannot live. My time is filled with continuous moments of joy in the things that I do, I still listen to music that I enjoyed listening to when on earth, but the music here is felt as well as heard, It seems to live and breath, and each note caresses my very being. I can still go to the theatre, where plays of morality and spiritual lessons are played out, and the whole audience absorbs the different uplifting stories. Some will make you laugh and cry, but not with tears of sadness, but with tears of emotional understanding.

I hope this letter finds you in good health and good spirits, for I know you just finished celebrating Christmas and the New Year. This is a time for you when you reflect on the old and the past, and resolve to do new things with a new attitude, a time to look forward.

I want you to know that I am with you always and that I hear your prayers, especially those you send for me, for they help me greatly. I was with you the other day, when you were feeling a little bit downhearted, and I tried my hardest to surround you with my love and get your attention. You thought you saw the teacup move, yes that was me, as you reached out and put your hand around the cup, I put my hand around yours, and for a moment we were together again. Please keep our memory alive, when you think that you have forgotten important times that we spent together, I will be there to jog your memory, a certain smell, a sound, a certain taste, will suddenly bring those memories flooding back, I am never far away from you. I know that I seem far away from you, but I am closer than I ever was, for I know your every thought, know how you are feeling and understand why, and know and understand your every action, that is how close I now am to you.

There is never a day that I do not know the joys and the heart-breaks that your life constantly deals out to you , I am on the roller coaster with you, and when it stops, and it's time for you to get off, I'll be there to stretch out my hand and help you off. So for now, take a deep breath and continue your life's journey, do the best that you can with what you have, give of yourself as often as you can, for one day you will be writing this letter of love from spirit, and hopefully you will be the object of someone's pleasant memory.

All my love always.

Your constant companion.

THE BATTLE CONTINUES

There is at the moment a battle going on in the world, a battle between positive and negative. This same battle is endured daily in our individual lives, we struggle daily over the negative and positive feelings that we have, and try hard to decide which thought or feelings we should listen to. It is a great battle indeed, for whichever direction we choose to follow, there is always a consequence, an effect, for that natural law of cause and effect, will play itself out no matter what. A positive action will have a positive effect, and equally a negative action will have a negative outcome or effect. You cannot plant the seeds of one flower and have it grow into an entirely different flower unexpectedly, that would be against the law of nature.

The laws of nature are the same spiritual laws that apply to mankind, of course there are man made laws, which are changed often according to how our ideas change, but not so with the laws of spirit. We each bring the laws of spirit into play by our actions and thoughts.

The future, your future, is not set in stone, you can change it at any time. We each have a goal, a reason for coming here, something to achieve. That goal is somewhere in the future, we may not even know what that goal is, but we can by our awareness and guidance from spirit, choose the road which is most likely to take us there. By some inner awareness, we know when we are on the wrong path, so we choose another, and always we are being watched and encouraged by our loved ones in spirit. It can sometimes feel a lonely road, but in that loneliness we are tapping into the spiritual resources that we have within us and our spiritual growth continues without our even realising it. Doors are opened for us so that we can have new experiences and new growth in spirit, the seeds that we have planted along the way, flower and bring us great benefits. The positive seeds that we plant now, will bring us positive benefits in the future, nothing is ever forgotten or wasted, for in life you reap the benefits of what you have sown. One day the harvest will come and your crop of spiritual food will be the sustenance that you have reaped for yourself. How big or small the harvest is, is in your hands, it can be a joyful day when the sun shines at it's brightest.

So take the road that will lead you to that wonderful harvest of your life, it may not necessarily be the easiest road or the smoothest, but your challenges you should meet with a positive force, for in life positive and negative are two sides of the same coin.

THE MARCH FOR PEACE

The world at the moment hangs on to hope, the hope that has become strengthened by many people coming together. The hearts of many have joined together to dispel a terrible humanitarian threat. The threat of war and human atrocity has caused people to think with their hearts, it will serve you well for now you know and have felt what love can do. Now you know what strength there is in love, for when love makes up its mind to act its strength cannot be weakened, its strength doubles and triples and spreads around the world. The stubborn cannot ignore it, its face is too large to turn away from and ignore, it looms in every direction that you turn, it will do its work, and in every space it will fill and spread until immersion is complete, for this is the quest of spirit, and we are spirit.

Whatever the outcome of that march for peace, whether war is averted or not, a demonstration of oneness of mind was shown, it matters not that the physical presence of some were lacking, but the positive thought and emotion joined with others both here and in spirit, to show the effect of positive force.

In your individual lives, this same positivity can be used for the good of others and yourselves. Do not keep it buried; uncover that same will and strength that seeks expression in every aspect of your life. As you give so you receive in abundance, not always is your reward physical but there are blessings that are worth far more than any material chattels and ornaments, blessings that can be kept for an eternity, there is no physical comparison to blessings and gifts from spirit, they are of the spirit and are without end and cannot deteriorate with age.

Look for those blessings in your life, there are more than you think, they go unrecognised for a long time until realisation comes with your spiritual growth, the eyes open and the truth of the life you live is revealed to you, in a wonderful moment of spiritual enlightenment. There will be many of these moments in your life as the road you travel helps you to visit them. Don't let these moments pass you by unnoticed, they are invaluable and will help to define who and what you are.

MEMORIES

It may seem as though there is not enough time to complete all that you wish to do, but be reassured that there is more than enough time allocated to each and every person, to do that which to them is important. Time is one of the biggest illusions that exist, it seems to creep up on you when you have a task to complete, or fast forward, making you feel that there is not enough time, but for all time, there is no end. It can seem to push you along and at other times stand still and hold you back. In reality, time has no beginning and no end that we know of.

Your daily routine will consume the hours of the day, in one way or another. If you value your time, you will fill your hours of the day doing things that mean something to you, and bring some form of enjoyment to others, for in time those that you associate with, will appreciate and remember the meaningful moments that you spent together, for our memories will be filled, and over the years will remember those moments when our hearts were made joyful by others, and the things we did.

At this time of the year, it is especially a memorable time when families and friends bring joy to each other; our hearts seem to open up and go out and embrace our loved ones, both here on earth and in the spirit world. Love seems to grow and is alive and felt by all. It is at this time of year especially that our loved ones in spirit draw close to us, for they are attracted by the loving thoughts and wishes that fill our hearts. They too want to share in those fond memories of past times when our families were all together, so when you lay the table this Christmas, know that there will be no empty chairs at your table, those that you loved and have gone before you to the Summerland, have not forgotten you, they are very much still a part of your life, and this season is no exception, if you can, let them know that you still welcome them at the table, raise a glass or two in tribute, that small gesture will help to fill their hearts even further with the joy that they remembered sharing with you in times gone by, and they will let you know one way or the other that they are still with you.

Past memories can sometimes be tinged with sadness, but let that sadness only last for a fleeting moment, for your loved one in spirit that sits beside you, wants you only to grasp the happiness from those times, and revel in the blessings that each new day brings, and for all your blessings, do not forget to give your thanks to the Divine Spirit and creator of eternal life.

WHAT HAPPENS AT THE END?

What happens at the end
When I close my eyes on this physical world?
Do I float away into nothingness
And become like a bird?
Do I sink into a dreamless sleep,
And become part of time?
Or do I step into another world
Where endless love is mine?

Will I find myself in a long dark tunnel
Searching for the light?
Or in a beautiful garden with springs and fountains
And colours that behold my sight?

Am I to become part of nature
And roam for evermore,
In the wind, through the trees and blades of grass,
In the flowers that feed the bees?

I don't yet know the answers
To these questions that I seek,
I've left it a bit late to make enquiry
So to speak,
It never seemed important when in years
I was young,
I would go on for ever, so I thought,
But I was wrong.

My body is now well worn,
And illness taken its toll,
This overcoat has had its day,
Away now it must fall.

My unseeing eyes now grow heavy,
And sleep now comes to me,
But what a joy it is
To see that light surrounding me.

Song and laughter, hugs and smiles,
My heart sings loud and clear,
They greet me with their outstretched hands,
All doubts now disappear.

That moment of reunion,
When hearts of love entwine,
A beautiful experience.
The plan was divine.

While living in the body of flesh,
It's important that you know,
That death is but an open door,
To those that went before.

SEEK PEACE AND HARMONY

There is nothing in your world that cannot be overcome once you have knowledge of spiritual truths. The time will come when this truth and knowledge will be spread across the earth, but in the meantime, there will be many wars, many sacrifices made in the process of that search for truth.

Truth and knowledge always comes in the aftermath of disturbance, as the light always follows the darkness, but come it will, it is part of the divine plan. The world seems to suffer great pains, but the mother too suffers pain in bringing forth a much loved child, this is how it will be until mankind learns that there is naught to be gained from harming one another. It is unfortunate that this knowledge has not yet been understood, but in the process of time, the lessons will be learned and lived. Peace and harmony are the world's heritage, you do not have to fight for it, and it is your right, given to you by the great and divine peacemaker. It was never His wish that strife should come to your world, but mankind has free will and that will is being used in the way that he feels it should. Power seems to be man's glory, greed his footstool, and until these are swept away, life will continue to be a battle. It is always going to be a battle between the material and the spiritual, mankind has chosen to learn the lesson the hard way, but the lesson must be learned no matter how long it takes.

There are spirit helpers that come to share knowledge of a spiritual nature with you, they can only give you the truths, you can choose whether or not to take it and use it for the benefit of the world, there will never be any force in the spreading of this knowledge, for by its very nature it is gentle and given in love. There is only one who can decide, you are personally responsible for what you do, and you are the higher of all God's creatures, having the ability to think rationally, you choose the darkness or the light.

We who come from the light are always near to help when you are in need, it is our wish that you live in peace and harmony, it is always your well-being that we have in mind when we come to you. It saddens us when we see the turmoil that the world is in, yes we can help you by our words of encouragement and the direction that we can give you, but the real work has to come from you, we cannot physically lead you; we cannot encroach on your free will. The realisation of the wrongs you do, have to come from you and the changes have to be made by you. The Divine Spirit will not stop you from destroying each other, your free will, will never be taken away from you, and there is no profit to be gained in turning you into robots with no will of your own.

You have no earthly master, but the power of the will which is the greatest gift given to each and every one of you to use freely. Learn to listen to your higher self promptings, this is your link to the only true master that there is, once you accustom yourself to this way of thinking, all the worldly wars will cease, for where there is light, the darkness cannot penetrate, seek to express love and light always, that is your destiny and a truth that will bring you all closer to harmony and peace.

THE LIGHT AT THE END OF THE TUNNEL

There is always light at the end of the tunnel. Even when that darkness seems to close in and grip you and the loneliness is loud and painful. The light, far away as it may seem is looming up quicker than you think, just hold on, hold on to the knowledge that your loved ones in spirit have now gathered around you, steady hands guide you and hold you up.

This difficult time, which you experience, will come to an end, for your spirit friends are busy influencing those around you who are connected with your situation, to bring about peace and an end to your pain. Your cries for help have been heard, you need now to listen for the reply and watch for the signs that they send you. When they send someone to you who can help, it is not a coincidence, when you meet a stranger who has knowledge of your situation, it did not happen by chance, and when someone hugs you for no apparent reason, who do you think directed them to do it?

Our loved ones in spirit will do everything in their power to make that connection with us, they will use whatever materials, or influence by their thoughts, whoever they can to help us, but most of the time we are totally unaware of these spirit workings, which are done purely out of love and not for any thanks at all. "is there anybody there?" we usually cry, in our darkest hour, when we are blindly stumbling about looking for that light, looking for that way out. If you cannot do anything else, if you have done all you can, there is only one thing left for you to do and that is to be still, within yourself and your mind. Allow them to reach you, to soothe you, when circumstances are beyond your control, use spirit as your lifeline and hold on. They will hold you up for as long as it takes, that dark cloud in your life, was just temporary, none of us live in perpetual darkness, that guiding light of spirit is always there, your vision may become clouded so that you cannot see it, but trust them, circumstances may even obscure that light, but it is there, waiting to lead you out of the woods into the countryside of happier times.

LET YOUR SPIRIT SHINE

There is within you a light that wants to shine, a light that wants to love, and a light that wants to create. That light within you is the spirit. It has not yet shined at its brightest, or loved all it can, or expressed all of its true feelings. It is longing to do a lot more of all of these things. In it's longing to do so, it becomes more agitated and frustrated in its wait for the right situation, when it can express itself. Occasionally the right situation does occur and it is suppressed and prevented from showing what it can do, indeed the moment passes, when for some reason fear prevented it from bursting forth. What have you to fear? The way is shown to you all the time, a kind word, a light touch, a smile of acknowledgement was all that was needed as a first step, little by little is just as good as a continuous flow of spiritual help and good wishes towards others. It need not be a gushing waterfall of niceties, but here and there just enough to make another smile. There will always be opportunity, but do not let fear of what others will think of you prevent your true expression of the spirit within, for your spiritual growth is yours alone, your responsibility and is in your hands.

You are writing your life's story, and you play the lead role in it. Those you have met along the way, are also writing their life's story and the different chapters will last as long as you want them to. This book, you will read at the end of your physical life here on earth, every detail of your life will be there written by your hand, your actions and reactions, your thoughts and words said, the laughter and the tears. There will be many different characters in this book of your life that had an effect on your behaviour, but in the end, your actions were your own, and the responsibility cannot be shifted to another.

Do you need to start a new chapter in your life? Is it time to turn over a new leaf? It's up to you, when you wake up tomorrow, what will you write on that new page? Hopefully it will be that you felt the stirrings of something new within you, as your spirit within awakened to a new realisation that the life you live from this day forward, can be your personal best seller, and the prize you win can be better than any earthly award, for as spirit always tell us, love is all there is, and there's plenty for everybody.

TODAY IS THE FIRST DAY OF THE REST OF YOUR LIFE

Today is the first day of the rest of your life, and tomorrow is the result of what you do today. If you take these words and try to live by them, you will never need to fear your future. You will learn to strive to live each day as though it is your last, putting all your strength into giving each moment meaning, for each day that you live would be special and enhanced by the beauty that you try to give to the moment.

It seems like hard work but it is not, if you understand that the future is connected to now, this moment in time. In spirit, there is no time; there is just the moment that is being lived which is most important. In the course of time here on the earth, there are events that continually take place in your lives and events that constantly seem to shake us privately and worldwide, but the illusion is that humanity takes each event and holds onto it for an eternity, creating history, as our books will show us, but letting go and learning from these events, and moving forward will create a new and uncompromising future. Today your experiences will stay with you as a memory naturally, but consciously letting go of them when hurtful or negative, if you perceive them as such, will release you from their hold and enable you to go forward with the rest of your life and into your future. Now is all that matters, it is not productive to constantly jump ahead in thought, with worries of things that may never happen and often don't. The future always takes care of itself, without even the slightest thought from you; it will always be there, even if you are not. The future cannot be prevented from happening, but it can be smoothed and directed by the thoughts and actions of today. Steer your lives into the great ocean of abundant and positive possibilities, there is much for you to achieve with you at the helm of your ship, guiding and steering. You will occasionally have to drop anchor and rest a while, and take in the aromas and smells of the beauties that surround you, but rest is sometimes necessary, even when it is forced upon you.

The future awaits every single one of you, but you must not fail in your duties to each other, to mankind. Each individual is a part of you, you are connected, be kind for in the future you may both need to depend on each other for help, and unity may be the only way of going forward.

Decide today that now is the only time that matters and that in the next moment your future will be secure and prosperous, for you will have already made it in your actions of loving kindness.

YOU ARE NOT ALONE

When the world around you feels as though it is falling in on you, and crumbling, and all your expectations and hopes feel as though they have been dashed, your natural reaction is to fall into the darkness of depression and despair. The isolation and loneliness that you feel is very real, but you must try and remember that you are not alone, for every tear that you shed is seen and felt by those in spirit who continue to share your life, and continue to love you.

You are not alone, for your sadness is theirs as is your laughter. They continually pledge never to leave you, especially in your hour of need. Talk to your loved ones at these times and they will come closer, their loving hands will be there to support you. This is not just an idle hope, it is a reality. They come here to prove this to us time and time again. Fight the depression that makes their presence more difficult to feel. The deeper you sink, the harder it is for them to reach you, as to them you are surrounded by a fog, and it will take longer for you to make your way up into the light of awareness. The darkness that surrounds you is only temporary, the clouds are not permanent, just as winter is not permanent, though it seems to hang around for a long time, soon it gives way to spring.

Their love is real and their help tangible. There is little that they can do if there is no effort coming from you, but in your striving, their help is there, you only need to ask. They know how difficult it is for us, for they once walked this earth and know how we are ruled and sometimes engulfed by our emotions, but the light and love of spirit is strong. The spirit within you is strong; we have not yet fully learnt how to tap into our own resources to gain that strength, and with the strength within combined with the strength of our loved ones, the upliftment can be life changing. There is always hope in every situation, no matter how dire we think it looks, for the surface of the problem is never the whole picture. Below the surface is always the new growth, the light that is fighting to get through, for the light will always eventually penetrate the darkness. Sometimes fighting the situation can make it worse, be still, within and without, let spirit do their work, let them help with their healing influence and listen to your feelings, sometimes those deep feelings are the answer to your prayers, communication from your spirit friends. Sometimes looking at a picture of your loved one in spirit, can make that connection stronger between you. They hear you and when the situation is resolved, give them your thanks for their help, for it is not an easy task that they have. To influence the heavy, dense minds of those of us here on earth takes a lot of effort and time, but their driving force is always love.

Take their blessings and their love, and strive to surmount all the difficulties that this life seems to throw at us from time to time, but remember our loved ones walk in our footsteps, and indeed sometimes they carry us.

THE RICHES OF SPIRIT

Seek out for yourselves, moments of peace and tranquillity, when you can still your mind and your emotions, in order to make that connection with those you love in spirit. It is in that peace that the veil between this physical world and the world of spirit can be drawn, open to those who seek to increase their knowledge of spirit, and for wisdom to be imparted. You do not have to be a medium to be able to do this, knowledge and wisdom is for all.

When the turmoil of this physical world gets too much, withdraw for a while, ask your loved ones for help, your spiritual battery will be topped up and you will feel once again re-energised enough to continue your daily lives. Feeling once again revived, you will be the one to offer yourself in service to others, you will be one of the many workers for spirit, for the kindness that you show to others, never goes unnoticed or unpaid, even when you feel it is so. The time will come for all when all our accounts will be balanced up, and all dues will be paid, hopefully all our accounts will be well balanced and hopefully you will be in credit, but know that all debts will have to be paid, large or small. If you know you have spiritual debts to pay, now is the time to pay them, it may cost you a little bit of pride, but that is something we all have in abundance while here on earth, but once you pass to spirit, the value of pride diminishes greatly. The more valued coins of spirit being truth, love and kindness, and all that is positive within you, can be displayed daily, these are the riches of spirit that last for all time, that are remembered and talked about and should be taught to the young, who have as yet little vision, for these coins of spirit, when shared, repay in kind.

So be rich in spirit, for wealth of spirit can be taken with you when you pass away from this earth, and it is a wealth that you can keep for all time, and wear in recognition of your achievements, not in an arrogant display, but in humility, knowledge and wisdom, you will claim all that is rightfully yours, and it will be granted to you freely and in love.

YOU REAP WHAT YOU SOW

There is a greater power,
That governs you and me,
He organised the universe
And set His children free.

He made the world in such a way
That love would make it grow,
From January to December,
Through the sunshine and the snow.

He gave us all a heart and soul,
And told us to be kind,
And tolerant towards those you meet
For you should bear in mind.....
That every soul is part of me,
And you are part of each other,
We are all one, like it or not,
You are sister and brother.

To cause another harm or hurt,
By some deliberate act,
You bring into action,
My universal law of life,
Cause and effect.

You cannot escape this eternal law,
It operates for all,
You cannot make a deal with Him,
Once you get the call......

To return to that life beyond
This material plane,
Where you are seen for who you are,
And there can be no blame.

You are the one, who lived your life,
It may be hard to admit,
He gave you lots of opportunities,
To make the best of it.

We make mistakes all the time,
Throughout our earthly life,
But here is the place to work and strive,
To try and put them right.

Untold pain is felt by those who
Realise another
Has been hurt by word or deed,
And caused that soul to suffer.

The perpetrator of that pain,
His eyes now open wide,
Can see and feel that pain inside,
From this he cannot hide.

With love and light I tell you,
It is better that you live,
To serve your fellow man
And learn to forgive.

In peace and harmony mankind can live,
And this you surely know,
Life gives back what you put in,
You reap what you sow.

YOUR PART IN THE BIGGER PLAN

There is a plan that has been formulated for this world and mankind. Each one of us are part of that plan, we each individually came to this earth plane with a plan, a plan that only you can achieve for yourself, yet is part of the greater worldly plan. Insignificant you are not, for creation has been continuing for millions of years, yet no matter what takes place in the world, good or bad, the world continues to revolve. The seasons continue to change and the sun continues to rise and set, but the part we play, as individuals are most important. You may think that your presence in this world counts for very little, but it is not so, you play a very big part in your family, without you it could not run as smoothly as it does, without you there would be a very large gap. You are needed to keep the wheels turning, there would be a disintegration of family values, were you not present. In the work that you do, you are again a small but important part of the whole, and so it is with the wider world, you are needed to complete the bigger picture, there will never be a time when individuality is not important. The part you play is your choice, you have choices of one kind or another to make every day, it is part of life, but never forget that those choices you make affect many other people. If your choice will do no harm to others, then know that you have made the correct one, if it creates harmony among others, then your choice will also benefit you.

Be aware of the choices that you make for they may be forgotten by you the moment after they have been made, but their effects you will feel at some future date, and more than one person may help you to remember. So in the choices that you make let harmony be your guide, so that the lessons of tolerance, patience and love will be easier to learn and appreciate, and you will have played your part in the greater plan.

WHAT IS SPIRITUALITY?

It is a word that we use so often within our daily lives to describe people or experiences, but what does it truly mean? It is an essence and expression of the soul within.

Every living person has a soul and a spirit, indeed we are all spirit possessing a soul and the soul within each of us, has different qualities of expression. If each of us could learn to express and connect with the soul within, then we would all go a long way to becoming spiritual beings. The soul does not comfortably express negative qualities. Our different lives have moulded each of us through our various experiences, whether good or bad, in our consideration, but the soul within each of us always seeks the light and truth within every situation, but occasionally, the physical mind through our various experiences, tends to mask the truth, and soul expression, and the expression of the soul's light, can become distorted.

There is light within all mankind, it was put there by the Divine Spirit, and we through our various life journeys are trying, and wish to be free from the trappings of physical life. Through life's lessons, we enter into a kind of sleep state where we seem to be unaware of what the spirit and soul try to tell us and in a way, ignore it's voice because of the physical life that we live, and the material life can totally obliterate the longings of the spirit within, but the awakening comes to us all eventually, usually through dark times or traumatic experiences that suddenly give us that big wake up call. That experience is physically unpleasant but the spirit within at that time, usually says, "Hi, I've been trying to talk to you for a while now, but you weren't listening, let me lead you along this bumpy road, I will lead you out of this darkness into the light, but you must heed my voice. I am the real you, it's time that our relationship became stronger". The spirituality within you, then gets the chance to shine through, that essence of the divine light then begins to have a voice through you and the light within begins to shine. And those around you begin to notice the difference. There then begins to be a calmness within you that you've never before experienced.

In your prayers you find a far reaching confidence, and your whole life begins to change. It all starts with you asking yourself, "What do I need to change about myself?" there isn't really anything to change, for you already have within you the soul and essence of love, you just need to open the door and greet it, and allow it to shine as it has always longed to do. Listen to the call of that inner voice, it will lead you to many great moments in your life, and will help you to realise that the boundaries that you set for yourself in life can be pushed further and further afield until you finally realise, there are no limits to your abilities and to what you can achieve.

65

ACKNOWLEDGE THE SPIRIT WITHIN

At some time in your life, the spirit within will be acknowledged, and with that acknowledgement, should come relevant action.

For a long time, that spirit that lies within us all lies dormant and inactive for the simple reason that awareness of its presence may be lacking. That spirit within, was called into being by the Divine Spirit that governs all life, within every physical vessel, there lies the true self, the soul and the spirit, you cannot have one without the other, for they are intertwined for eternity.

Eternity cannot be fathomed with the physical brain, but nevertheless, they will always be. Your physical expressions are determined by the condition of spiritual development of your soul. You act according to your soul development, and when the soul attains a high development in spiritual understanding, your spirit and physical bodies will always act accordingly. Always remember, that spirit is the superior and the physical body the lower, which learns to be the obedient pupil. Can the physical body on its own, rise to the state of a master? No, always the spirit dictates according to its level of spiritual attainment.

The soul, created by the Divine Father, enters physical life on its journey of growth. Since we all have the same Father and creator, so we are all brothers and sisters in spirit, regardless of physical shortcomings, which are only temporary, for if you desire that spiritual growth strongly enough, nothing of this physical earth, can stand in your way.

Willpower, is a gift that was instilled in every soul, when used for the good of self and others, it is indeed a power that can overcome even the highest of hurdles. It is a power when used rightly, which can cause seeming mountains to move out of your way, and paths to be cleared, in ways that can seem miraculous. The power of the spirit is one that is not nebulous, but of light, and all that is positive.

Let light forever be in your souls, beckon it to you at every opportunity, and you will find that the result will only enhance every part of your being, both physically and spiritually. That is the loving power that the creator extends to you all. The power of spirit always gives with love.

ALL ARE WORTHY OF HIS LOVE

Many times in our lives, we will feel dejected, rejected and alone. These are very common human feelings, that all people experience and feel at some time, whether through situations that have come upon us, or through talking ourselves into these feelings, they are still very painful and debilitating.

It is whilst being in this negative cloud, that we can learn a lot about ourselves and others. When coming across someone in this experience, the desire to help them out of this cloud becomes very intense, and this is when our friends in spirit move in with their strong influences, to bring comfort to those who are suffering, either mentally or physically. They can create an atmosphere of peace around you with their loving thoughts, and assert the very positive powers of healing.

Mental stress is very much a hidden pain, and the sufferer can feel very low, whilst showing to the world a face of contentment. What you feel inside, is very much what your loved ones in spirit see and concern themselves with, that is where the real persona resides, and it cannot be hidden from them.

You are loved, no matter what wrongs you have done, or perceive yourself to have done, it is always spirits love for you that brings them to you. You are not an island in a vast ocean, but a grain of sand amongst many others, each grain being known and loved by The Divine Spirit equally. Each grain has a different shape, weight and colour, but with one common destination and worth. We have one creator, and all are worthy of His love, all are here for one purpose, to be an individual among many, and to enhance the lives of all those that come into your space, one grain of sand cannot make a beach, as one person alone cannot change the world, but you can make a difference, cause a ripple, draw the attention of others with the positive things that you do, it need not be anything big, in terms of change, but a word, a helping hand, these are the little things that have meaning to the few and collectively, cause mountains to move.

Your eyes do not deceive you when you see the miracle in a birth and in physical death, for they are both beginnings, and a new start to a journey of spiritual growth. Your sadness too is part of that journey, but do not hold it close, let it go with the wind, and allow joy to take its place within you.

LOVE IN ACTION

Sometimes in our lives, we find ourselves in a situation that just will not go the way we want it to go. Most of us like to be in control of our lives and what is going on in it, but occasionally, we feel our of control, as though things are snowballing and getting worse, and we are totally at a loss as to how to stop it.

In situations like this, you have to say well, I've done all I can now, and I have to give this situation over to that greater power in the universe, The Divine Spirit, God, for only higher hands can now help.

Suddenly people start to cross your path that you have never met before, and turn out to be just the right person, and begin to offer to help you out. Their presence in your life came about at just the right time. I wonder who could have sent them to you. You may suddenly start seeing articles in the newspaper, phone numbers or addresses, which are just what you need for your problem.

You will begin to meet people, who went through the same thing you are going through, and there you have a supporting friend who can offer advice. There is no limit to the many ways that our spirit friends and loved ones can help us, to us it will seem like a miracle, but to our spirit friends, it is another opportunity for them to smooth our path for us and uplift us, and this they love to do, for they want to see us happy.

It is always within their ability, and is constant proof that we are not alone in our lives, and that they walk with us through our many ups and downs. It takes only a moment to give them your thanks, for the help they give us; they like to feel your loving appreciation, not because of any need, but just to be acknowledged.

Their work and help, is based on love and that love comes from a higher source than them, and if you are benefited in any way by the love in action that they have shared with you, then they are happy to have been of service to you, for it is ultimately God whom they serve, and by working with and helping those they can on the earth plane, that service changes and transforms their souls.

So let us all realise, that the love and service we receive from our loved ones in spirit must be passed on in love and service to those we meet in our daily lives, and thus the chain of love and service to The Divine Spirit can continue in both worlds. As you receive, so you must give, making sure that you who represent one link in the chain, becomes strengthened and blessed, for every link in that chain, is known and loved by The Divine Spirit.

HIS LOVE IS ALL EMBRACING

Each and every one of you is a child of God, created by The Divine Spirit in love and wisdom, not by any kind of mistake or accident, but with purpose, reason and meaning.

Each of you has a spirit and a soul with a destiny that lies before you, seemingly unknown, but there nevertheless. With each thought, deed and action, your destiny can be altered in a positive or negative way, according to the way you think, for what you view as negative, usually has a beneficial outcome in the long run.

The power that created you, knows your strengths and your weaknesses, and smiles upon you when both are demonstrated, for a parent always watches his children with pride and knowledge, knowing that they grow through experience and sometimes frustration. We are children of many colours, but connected by the same spirit, it saddens us all when we cannot live side by side in peace, but we continue to have hope in the knowledge that we can turn to our creator, without fear, and be loved unconditionally, for the love of a parent for his child, is the strongest of all loves.

You cannot ever be alone, for that would mean that you have been forgotten, and the wisdom and love of which I speak, cannot make a mistake. You are in the hands and charge of those unseen, but real, who have a duty to watch and care for you throughout your earthly life, and let us not forget those who when they were here, had a blood bond also and still continue that bond of love whilst in the world of spirit. There is no disconnection because of physical death.

No, you cannot be alone for His love is all embracing and reaches even those who wish to hide themselves away, in time, even they will see that their loneliness was a misguided thought. So keep your thoughts positive as often as you can, when those negative thoughts threaten to fill your mind, actively push them away, you are strong enough to achieve this and anything that you wish to achieve in your life.

Your thoughts and ideas of a positive future for yourself will fan out and touch and affect others, in this way, you become a teacher for others, and as you teach, those listening and watching, will follow in your positive footsteps, and the chain reaction will continue.

We who were all created in love, as children of The Divine Spirit, let us join together and become a positive force in the lives of others and the world.

SPIRITUAL COMPANIONS

There isn't a day that goes by
That our loved ones don't try
To inspire and communicate their love,
But our minds seem so closed
To the words they unfold,
And a deaf ear we turn once again.

They will never give up
Trying to cheer us up,
So the words they will plant in our minds,
And just when you think
You are ready to sink,
The situation does a complete turnaround.

Well how did that happen?
We are heard to say often,
When things were looking so grim,
Off course it was them
Coming to the rescue again,
When in trouble they never desert us.

Your mother, your father,
Your son and your daughter,
Your uncle, aunt and grandparents,
Want nothing more
Than to let you know,
They still love you and are
Around and about us.

Their lives did not end,
At the graveside my friend,
They return again and again,
To guide you and keep you
On the pathway that's good for you,
Until the day that you all REUNITE.

BECOME AT PEACE WITH YOURSELF

It seems that many of you have so much time to give to others, but very little time for yourselves.

While giving of yourself is very helpful and honourable, it is important to know that each and every one of you is a unique soul and spirit, whose self development is of extreme importance, and that you need time out from your busy lives and people.

Solitude is something that very few of you seek for, yet it is in that solitude that you can find many of the answers that you seek. It can also refresh and refuel the spirit for difficult times ahead, and once you learn to withdraw from the hustle and bustle of life, it can truly become your life-line to spirit.

In the silence there are many loved ones from the world of spirit who can draw close to you, and give you much needed help, strength and healing. Your thoughts and prayers now focused, can rise upon the ether and be acted upon with the love that you desire. At these times reach out with your heart and mind, and with the confident thought that you are heard. It does not matter your age or your gender, the love and tenderness of spirit is there for all to use.

Practice becoming one with spirit, you will then become at peace with yourself, and when that happens, problems will cease to look so big in your life, since your guides and helpers will draw ever closer to you, and you will become attuned on a level that you can both work together, for the good of yourself and others.

There is never any need to fret, for fear is mankind's worst enemy. In your hearts there is strength so far untapped, constantly spirit try to release this strength within you, but fear and anguish always seem to get in the way. This blockage is hard to remove, but the love of spirit always overcomes eventually.

Be strong in thought and mind, it will help you to advance along the path of life. Never forget that you do not tread your path alone, for every hurdle that you come up against, diminishes in size with each one that you clear.

Put any problem that you have in a tiny box, for in reality they are not as big as you perceive them to be, and when you feel overwhelmed by them, give them to spirit and they will hold them for a while until you regain your strength to deal with them, and with the sunshine of spirit upon your back, the battle will be won before it is even fought.

TRUTH NEVER CHANGES

Mankind has many laws that change and adapt to the moral thoughts of the day, and as man evolves, the laws will also change to accommodate the ideas of the changing times. New laws are brought in or just not used, as they become old and inappropriate, but this is not so with the laws of The Divine Spirit, for God's laws and truths remain eternal, and have always been and will always be.

The law of cause and effect has and will always be. The law of do unto others as you would have them do unto you, will always remain, and the effect of breaking such laws, still remains the same no matter how evolved mankind becomes. The laws of fire, water, wind and rain will always be the same, for nature too has to obey and work within certain laws.

If all the laws of nature were suddenly withdrawn, there would be no structure within which these elements could function, and the planet would be devastated, and we would live in constant fear of being struck by lightening or consumed by fire each time we stepped out of our doors. There are laws which govern every event, even our own bodies are abiding by certain laws every minute of the day in order for us to live.

The laws and truths of spirit, demand that we as spirit evolve into higher beings provided that we obey certain laws, and it is up to us as individuals, to try and put these spiritual laws into practice daily. If we could have our spirit eyes opened for just a few moments of time, we would truly understand the consequences of all our actions, whether positive or negative, the trouble is that as materialistic people living in a very slow and materialistic world, realisations are slow to come to us, and we have to endure the slow progress that an earthly body has to face, but truth is never far from us and its discernment always within our ability.

If we make the decision to follow the path that spirit have directed us to, we will discover that the truth and ability to discern it is within us all, the problem is we tend to waver and often deliberate unnecessarily, when we know the truth. If in your heart you can become closer to God the Divine Spirit, then truth will never desert you, and you will always be in its presence, and all those whom you serve will know that you walk and abide in truth.

THE WHEEL OF CIRCUMSTANCE

Enjoy the life that you are living, for it is only a moment in eternal years.

The life on earth which stretches ahead of you may seem long, but as you get older and you become more mature and experienced, the years seem to pass you by with a much greater speed. Each moment lived should be grasped with both hands, and every bit of joy should be squeezed out of it for yourself.

If a situation that you are in does not seem particularly positive, then find a way to make the outcome joyous for someone else, for one day when looking back on your life, you will be able to say, I did it for them, and that will bring you joy indeed.

Far too often we tend to look for faults in people or in what they are doing, but when we do that we are setting in motion a negative wheel of circumstances, which will surely trample and mow down any positive seeds that may have been sown. Every person has at least one positive seed within them, it may still be in the darkness beneath the soil, but if you can shine that light of positivity upon them, that seed will always grow towards your light, always try to be that light of encouragement.

You have that light and power within you, it has been given to us all freely, to use in whatever way you wish, and each time it is used positively, it increases and is always replaced when you feel your energy is depleted.

The Divine Spirit knows that life is not all roses, but the scent of that rose should remind you of your spiritual nature and capabilities. The painful and irritating thorns of life, will come in and out of your life like the occasional cloud passing over the sun, it is only dark for a short while, but the sun is always there waiting for its opportunity to shine, and shine it always does, but do not concentrate and focus on the rainy day, rather look forward to the inevitable sunshine, which brings with it a smile and an uplifted heart.

That positive wheel of circumstance will continue to turn, spurred on by your positive energy, keep it turning, remembering that your wheel of life continues to turn beyond this physical life, it can also be your wheel of spiritual fortune. The choice is yours.

I AM WITH YOU NOW AND ALWAYS

Are you already beset by memories of past Christmases, when they seemed to be happier times, more fulfilling and joyful than of more recent Christmases that you remember? Were those past Christmases more meaningful because of those loved ones who were present and are now sadly not physically here to share your laughter, hugs and kisses? Are you at this time feeling rather sad for the way you think Christmas should be, and cannot seem to bring that magic back into the festivities of this special time?

Well I may just be describing how you are feeling right now, but just take a moment to think about the reality of this special time. You may not physically have with you those from your past who seemed to make your Christmas time special, but they are there, even as your memory is cast back to those special moments in time, your loved ones in spirit sit with you and reminisce, for they have the same memories as you.

There will always be this trip down memory lane for you, perhaps this is the first time you are making it in this way, but you are not alone in making it. The tinsel, the songs, the baking, they do not need to be a memory that cannot be regained, better think that all your future Christmases will be spent with the two worlds, of spirit and this physical world coming together, and celebrating together as one, make that conscious decision to mentally include your loved ones, who to you seem gone and lost but in reality are by your side with their arms around your shoulders, laughing and enjoying your excited shouts of glee, and toasts of the season as you raise your glasses.

Do not forget to toast the one who sits in that empty chair, for it appears empty but is occupied by that friend and love from memory lane. To them you are an open book of which the pages of your life are still being written, it is time to make a new entry on this fresh page and today it will read, my loved one and I together walked a new road of experience, for everything I did today I knew he/she was with me, we held hands and I was greatly comforted in the knowledge that they were with me, and when the day ended and I said good night, I felt a tear of joy come to my eye, for he/she finally knew that I had realised what he/she had tried so long to let me know. I Am With You Now And Always.

GO FORWARD WITH NEW ASPIRATIONS

There is nothing more certain in our lives, than the fact that one day we shall all leave this physical world, adorned in our spirit bodies, to continue our lives in the world of spirit. Whether we experience that world as heaven or not, depends upon our actions and interaction with those we meet throughout our earthly lives.

Once we have passed over that threshold into the spirit world, there can be no more hiding, we shall all be seen for who we truly are. There will be no hiding behind different religions or faiths, no earthly title will allow you any special favours, all untruths will be revealed, and in our nakedness of character and true being, we will all stand. The spiritual aspects of your nature will shine, but any darkness of character will become apparent to all by your countenance, for at a glance all will know your story.

Since Spiritualism teaches us this truth, do we try with all our might each day to make sure that when we make that transition, our earthly story is one of, tried very hard and accomplished many difficult missions, or, overcame many hurdles through trial and error, but always kept his/her focus on the light at the end of each tunnel, for this life is the testing time, with many opportunities to achieve that spiritual accolade for personal achievements, in difficult conditions.

When opportunities pass us by, they usually return in a different situation. Put behind you those moments of disappointment where you think you failed, a new day, a new minute, a new hour has begun, go forward with new aspirations and determinations, for the road of progress stretches long and bright before you and with renewed will, all the treasures of spirit can be yours, but remember, the treasures spoken of are of the spirit, they are not material, if you pursue material treasures you will find that they are only for a season, of the earth earthly, and when you come to spirit you will find that your material mind binds you to your earthly treasures.

The treasures of the spirit are eternal and increase with your spiritual progress, be aware that you cannot serve them both (the material and the spiritual), but free will is yours to peruse as you desire, for there lies the key, your hearts desire can open up for you a future life of happiness or a life full of regrets and inner pain, but whichever you choose, spiritual progress remains eternally at your door to grasp at your will.

YOUR CREATION WAS A DELIBERATE ACT OF LOVE

Always remember that you, as a soul were first created in the world of spirit. Your creation was no mistake, but a deliberate act of love. As a soul you were given consciousness, awareness and an individuality and uniqueness that no other soul has. Yes, no other soul was made the same as you. That in itself is a miracle of life.

Since you were created by that great soul who is love, then within you is the capability to love and to increase that love. When you come from love and you allow that love to do its work, it can only grow. Your creator constantly surrounds you with His love, as a father and mother always does and constantly keeps you in His sights watching and wanting to protect you, but the child must always try to keep that connection of love whether in thought or prayer.

Our Divine Father has many children, whom He never stops loving, but some of His children feel lost and alone and have forgotten in the earth life that there is a reservoir of healing, love and upliftment that they can seek and turn to whenever they are in need of consolation. You are the loving child of His care, who has a myriad of workers in spirit who know and love you also and always have your interests at heart.

There is a long chain of spirit people that link back to the Divine Father, of people that have an interest in you, every link or person in that chain is known by someone higher up in that chain, for the higher always look after the lower, and there is always someone to turn to for advice and knowledge, you have many friends.

As a flower in a flower bed, your presence adds to the beauty of that bed as each individual flower does, you are needed, but do not allow yourself to be choked by the weeds of life, blocking out the very sun that gave you life, the weeds in your life can be controlled by never letting them overpower your life, and there is always someone stronger than you in spirit who you can trust to help keep the flower bed free from undesirables, there is help when you call, for life whether on the earth or in spirit is lived under the watchful eye of the Divine Spirit with eternal love, that calls for you His child and awaits your reply and acknowledgement.

SPREAD THE LOVE OF SPIRIT AROUND THE GLOBE

In a few days time, we will celebrate Christmas day, by giving gifts to our loved ones and eating more food than we would normally consume, because it is Christmas day. Churches all over the world will praise and celebrate the birth of one man who lived, preached and died on a cross over 2,000 years ago. This man named Jesus brought us a message of love and peace. He was a medium and healer who taught us also to love each other as brothers and sisters, for indeed we all have one Father and one creator, we are all spirit and linked by the hand that created us.

The world longs for love and peace, both globally and individually and suffers much in its attempts to bring it into being, but we must never stop trying. The spiritual path of each and every one of us must reflect that peace and brotherhood, for nations are made up of individuals.

One single thought, one single act of love towards another, may not make many waves, but when nations act in this way towards another, the ripples continue like the never ending circles caused when a stone is dropped into a still lake. The love within the heart and soul of man needs to be activated and used to make the waves that will be used to spread the love of spirit around the globe.

Time is continuous and there is no time like the present, for your spiritual welfare to be upgraded, never forget about the control that you have over self, you are your own master and your spiritual growth and direction is in your hands. Let each gift that you receive this Christmas help you to recognise the true spiritual gifts that you have already been given, for they are many and are often forgotten in the life of material living, and let each gift that you give, be a sharing of the love that the creator put in your heart at your creation.

Your loved ones in spirit draw ever closer at this time of year, celebrating with you, they all want to be remembered and are also a part of that circle of love, their messages of upliftment continue throughout the year, and so, as was the first message, let love, peace and harmony reign in your life now and eternally.

A DEDICATION TO MOTHERS IN SPIRIT

All my life I loved you
But didn't always say it,
I knew you'd always be there,
I took your love for granted.

Your caring and your sharing ways,
Soon rubbed off on me,
You taught me how to feely love
My own family

Always give without the thought
of receiving in return,
I watched you demonstrate this
many times, with the little you earned.

When I was down or hurt,
You always had wise words for me,
You'd talk me through my problems
And you made me clearly see.

That nothing was ever half as bad
As I imagined it,
You had a magic way of helping
All the darkest clouds to lift.

These memories I treasure,
For they are worth far more than gold,
A mother's love is priceless,
And in my heart I'll always hold.

A gratitude and thanks
For showing me the basic steps,
Of how to live with others,
No matter how hard it gets.

And even though you've passed
Into the other life to come,
I know that you can hear me
When I say, I Love You Mum.

THE GIFT OF LOVE

In a world that is currently full of strife and negativity, it seems hard sometimes to notice and appreciate the positive vibrations of love that do penetrate the darkness of our world. The words of love and peace that constantly emanate from our unseen friends and loved ones in spirit do occasionally, and more often than we think, reach us causing us to be calm and free from fear when we most need it.

Christmas time is no exception, the joy that is normally absent in our daily lives spreads throughout the land, in an ever increasing cloud, building a blanket of positive energy for all to feel and experience. It causes upliftment and smiles, even in the darkest of corners that usually seem untouched by love. Children dance and sing more loudly than usual, parents are more tolerant than usual, surrounding beauties seem to stand out and become more noticeable, the blue sky looks even more blue when the sun shines, for this is the time of year when a cold wind can make you feel a little less amenable towards others, but the overtaking sense of Christmas spirit will melt any feelings of discomfort.

At this time of year, there are many gifts exchanged, but there is one gift from spirit that costs nothing and is given to us freely, it is available to us every day of the year, and it falls into our laps unannounced and without ceremony, and that gift is love. I know you are not surprised by this revelation, for you hear that this is given to you weekly in your services, and as it is given to you, so you should also give it freely. It truly is the only thing that you can give away and become rich, not in earthly riches, but spiritual riches. With each gift you give this Christmas, make sure there is plenty of love wrapped up inside.

The gifts you receive this Christmas, may not be many in number, but can be spiritually multiplied many times over if the right thoughts are used. Do not forget that your thoughts and the motive and reasoning behind those thoughts affect those that they are directed to. In thought and deed, send your love and be fruitful, for the gift of love you send today will undoubtedly be yours in the future.